gourmet
food
for a fiver

gourmet
food
for a fiver

jason atherton
with judy joo

photography by yuki sugiura

Quadrille
PUBLISHING

notes

All spoon measures are level unless otherwise stated:
1 tsp = 5ml spoon; 1 tbsp = 15ml spoon.

All herbs are fresh and all pepper is freshly ground unless otherwise
suggested.

Stock recipes are provided (see pages 186–7), but you can use bouillon
cubes for convenience and to stay within budget if preferred.

Use free-range or organic large eggs unless otherwise suggested. If you
are cooking for anyone who is pregnant or in a vulnerable health group,
avoid those recipes that contain raw egg whites or lightly cooked eggs.

Buy unwaxed citrus fruit if you are using the zest, if possible.

Oven timings are for fan-assisted ovens. If you are using a conventional
oven, increase the temperature by 10–15°C (or 1 Gas Mark). Individual
ovens can deviate by as much as 10°C from the setting, either way. Get to
know your oven, always preheat it and use an oven thermometer to check
its accuracy.

Timings are provided as guidelines, with a description of colour and/or
texture where appropriate, but as ovens and hobs vary, the reader should
rely on their own judgement as to when a dish is properly cooked.

A few years ago, when the financial world collapsed and everyone tightened their belts I knew that the restaurant industry would suffer and that entertaining at home would become a more regular affair. As a chef and lover of artisan food, I dreaded Britain regressing to the 70s and 80s, when so many on limited budgets ate packaged frozen foods and everything with chips. But we, as a nation, have made huge gastronomic strides since then. Some of the world's finest chefs are working in Britain today and home cooking has become much more adventurous. The media has played an influential role, too, making cooking more accessible, fun and mainstream.

As soon as a recession begins, everyone starts telling you how to save money. You'll find bookshops crammed with cookery books based around frugal food – predictable pasta recipes, endless variations on jacket potatoes and other boring, bland ways to fill your stomach. I see things differently. Inexpensive food can – and should – be exciting, beautiful and delicious. Cook with the seasons – making the most of ingredients when they are at their best and least expensive – and you will eat well. Good food doesn't stem from big wallets. My motivation for this book is to show everyone, including those on a tight budget, that you can entertain with style for comparatively little.

Choose a starter and main course, or a main course plus dessert from this collection and you'll be able to serve up a fantastic meal for less than £5 a head. Or you may wish to go the whole hog and serve a three-course meal, which will cost a bit more but won't exactly leave you feeling strapped for cash. Of course you can easily up the quantities if you're serving more than four. Conversely, if it's dinner for two, most of the recipes can be halved successfully. Have a look at my menu suggestions (on pages 10–13).

One thing I can promise is that you won't find any mundane run-of-the-mill recipes here. Having travelled extensively and worked in many different countries, I'm fortunate enough to be able to draw on culinary inspiration from all over the world. With many of the recipes, I have applied exciting flavour combinations that I've discovered abroad to our home-produced ingredients. I have also used inexpensive cuts of meats where possible, such as beef flank, pork belly and lamb shoulder, which are generally much more tasty than the prime cuts. Similarly, I've selected some varieties of fish that are often overlooked and considered unappetising, such as pollock, mackerel and gurnard. Prepared and cooked in the right way with appropriate flavourings, these forgotten treasures will have you salivating.

You'll find some of the recipes familiar in their title, but not in their execution and presentation. Where I have included classic dishes, these are given a modern twist. My goal has been to offer you dishes that are interesting, full of flavour and exquisitely presented, yet all within reach financially. Whether you are entertaining friends or cooking a special family meal, you will find plenty to choose from, and many of the recipes are easily adapted to serve an intimate meal for two.

My mantra is simple – buy fresh, seasonal, and local where possible, and eat well, without busting the bank.

my ideal larder

THIS IS A LIST OF STORECUPBOARD INGREDIENTS THAT YOU'LL NEED TO PREPARE THE RECIPES
IN THIS BOOK. IT'S A FAIRLY BASIC INVENTORY AND YOU WILL PROBABLY FIND YOU HAVE MOST
OF THE ITEMS ALREADY IN STOCK.

Oils and vinegars

Olive oil

Sesame oil

Vegetable oil (or other neutral oil)

Balsamic vinegar

Red wine vinegar

Rice vinegar

Sherry vinegar

White wine vinegar

Spices, dried herbs and flavourings

Cardamom pods

Cayenne pepper

Chilli flakes

Cinnamon sticks (also ground)

Cloves

Coriander seeds (also ground)

Cumin seeds (also ground)

Mustard seeds

Nutmeg

Paprika

Pepper (black, white, pink peppercorns)

Saffron strands

Star anise

Bay leaves (freshly picked or dried)

Oregano

Bouillon cubes (chicken, fish, beef, lamb,
vegetable)

Sea salt

Tamarind paste

Vanilla extract

Baking

Baking powder

Brown sugar

Caster sugar

Cocoa powder

Cornflour

Cream of tartar

Flour (plain, strong plain and self-raising)

Granulated sugar

Icing sugar

Condiments

Chilli sauce

Fish sauce

Honey

Ketchup

Maple syrup

Mayonnaise

Mustard (Dijon and wholegrain)

Soy sauce

Tabasco sauce

Worcestershire sauce

Cooking wine

White wine (dry white)

Red wine (such as Côte du Rhône)

Note: These items have not been taken into
account in the overall costing of the recipes
as they are considered essential to the home
larder and are mostly used in small quantities.

MENU SUGGESTIONS

You'll probably want to pick and choose dishes to put together, but I thought I'd offer some suggestions for different seasons, occasions and cuisine styles, which work really well. Just drop a starter or dessert off any of the three-course ideas to bring your dinner under a fiver.

SPRING MENU

JERSEY ROYALS WITH AVOCADO, SMOKED TROUT AND HORSERADISH CREAM (PAGE 27)

SEA BREAM WITH TOMATO AND CORN SALSA (PAGE 58)

PINK PEPPERCORN MERINGUES WITH LEMON AND LIME CURD (PAGE 151)

SPRING TWO-COURSE MENU

CHILLED CUCUMBER SOUP WITH SALMON TARTARE (PAGE 22)

BRAISED LAMB WITH PEAS, BROAD BEANS AND CELERIAC PURÉE (PAGE 101, SHOWN LEFT)

SUMMER MENU

SUMMER CHERRY TOMATOES WITH CRAB SALAD (PAGE 28)

ROASTED CHICKEN WITH TUSCAN BREAD SALAD (PAGE 110)

STRAWBERRY SUNDAE (PAGE 120)

SUMMER TWO-COURSE MENU

POACHED POLLOCK WITH NIÇOISE SALAD AND AÏOLI (PAGE 65)

THYME-SCENTED STRAWBERRIES WITH MELON SOUP AND STRAWBERRY SORBET (PAGE 127)

AUTUMN MENU

BUTTERNUT SQUASH SOUP WITH CRAYFISH AND LIME CHANTILLY (PAGE 40)

BRAISED LAMB WITH IMAM BAYILDI AND BLACK OLIVES (PAGE 116)

PLUM AND APPLE BRUSCHETTA WITH CRÈME FRAÎCHE (PAGE 128)

AUTUMN TWO-COURSE MENU

STEAK AND POLENTA CHIPS WITH ROCKET AND PARSLEY PESTO (PAGE 102)

BAKED APPLES AND SULTANAS (PAGE 144)

WINTER MENU

ROASTED BEETROOT WITH BABY CHARD, GOAT'S CHEESE AND WALNUTS (PAGE 24)

PORK CHOPS WITH BLACK PUDDING AND APPLE (PAGE 113)

RICE PUDDING WITH WINTER FRUIT COMPOTE (PAGE 139)

WINTER TWO-COURSE MENU

CONFIT DUCK LEGS WITH ORANGE, GINGER AND WATERCRESS (PAGE 114)

CRÈME BRÛLÉE WITH PRUNES IN ARMAGNAC (PAGE 162)

VERY SPECIAL OCCASION

SALMON WITH PEA MOUSSE AND CRAYFISH TAILS (PAGE 43)

BRAISED LAMB WITH PEAS, BROAD BEANS AND CELERIAC PURÉE (PAGE 101)

VANILLA PANNA COTTA WITH TOMATO AND PASSION FRUIT SYRUP (PAGE 154, SHOWN RIGHT)

ASIAN FLAVOURS

SPICED GREEN PAPAYA AND ROASTED PEANUT SALAD (PAGE 31)

GRILLED SALMON STEAK WITH GINGER CHILLI GLAZE AND STICKY RICE (PAGE 70)

SPICED PINEAPPLE WITH COCONUT SORBET AND CANDIED GINGER (PAGE 136)

SPANISH FLAVOURS

GAZPACHO (PAGE 17)

PAELLA OF CHICKEN, SQUID AND CHORIZO (PAGE 89)

POACHED AUTUMN FRUITS IN WARM SANGRIA (PAGE 132)

VEGETARIAN MENU

GRILLED MEDITERRANEAN VEGETABLE SALAD WITH GOAT'S CHEESE (PAGE 35)

PASTA IN MUSHROOM SAUCE WITH POACHED EGG AND WHITE ASPARAGUS (PAGE 36)

SPICED CHOCOLATE CAKE WITH MACERATED RASPBERRIES (PAGE 177)

SHARING PLATTER... IDEAL FOR TWO

TOMATO SALAD WITH CARAMELISED ONION AND BLUE CHEESE (PAGE 21)

GURNARD WITH OLIVES AND ARTICHOKES (PAGE 79)

WHITE CHOCOLATE CUSTARD WITH RASPBERRIES (PAGE 171)

SHARING PLATTER... IDEAL FOR TWO

GRILLED MEDITERRANEAN VEGETABLE SALAD WITH GOAT'S CHEESE (PAGE 35)

LAMB STEAKS WITH POMEGRANATE, AVOCADO AND ARABIC BREAD (PAGE 94)

PEACH MELBA (PAGE 124)

QUICK AND EASY

SPICY PRAWN CAKES WITH A SPRING ONION GARNISH (PAGE 39)

GRILLED CHICKEN WITH TAMARIND AND HERB SALAD (PAGE 90)

YOGHURT WITH APRICOTS, HONEY AND PISTACHIOS (PAGE 131)

savoury

TO PLATE

Pour the gazpacho into individual bowls and drizzle with a little olive oil. Arrange the cucumber, radishes and tomatoes in each soup plate, top with some croûtons and drizzle with olive oil. Each guest pours the gazpacho into their soup plate at the table.

Gazpacho

6 tomatoes (about 450g), roughly chopped
3 black peppercorns
250–300ml tomato juice
4 basil sprigs, leaves picked
1 red pepper, halved, cored and deseeded
½ small yellow pepper, cored and deseeded
olive oil, to drizzle
1 garlic clove, peeled and chopped
1 thyme sprig, leaves picked

1 bay leaf
sea salt
2 tsp balsamic vinegar, or to taste

GARNISH:
2 slices of white bread, crusts removed
6–8 radishes
¼ cucumber
12 cherry tomatoes, halved

---

1 Mix the chopped tomatoes, peppercorns, 250ml tomato juice and about half of the basil leaves together in a large bowl. Cover and chill.

2 Cut the sweet peppers roughly into julienne strips. Heat a drizzle of olive oil in a large frying pan over a medium-low heat. Toss in the peppers along with the garlic, thyme, bay leaf, remaining basil and a few pinches of salt. Sauté gently for 8–10 minutes, without browning, until the peppers are wilted and soft. Remove from the heat and tip into the bowl of tomatoes. Mix well, then cover and leave to marinate in the fridge for 24 hours.

3 The following day, purée the soup in a blender until smooth; you may need to do this in batches. Pass through a fine sieve into a bowl, pressing the pulp with the back of a wooden spoon to extract all of the juice.

Season with salt to taste. Add the balsamic vinegar and a drizzle of olive oil to taste. If the gazpacho seems too thick, thin it by stirring in some more tomato juice. Cover and chill well.

4 To make the croûtons for the garnish, preheat the oven to 150°C/Gas 2. Cut the bread into 5mm cubes and toss with a generous drizzle of olive oil and a good pinch of salt. Scatter on a baking tray and toast in the oven until crisp and golden, about 3–4 minutes; set aside.

5 Clean the radishes well, keeping the roots and green tops intact, and cut each one crossways into 3 pieces. Toss in olive oil and salt. Cut the cucumber in half, then slice into crescents. Drizzle with olive oil and salt.

6 Before serving the gazpacho, taste and adjust the seasoning and pour into a jug.

THE SUCCESS OF THIS SOUP DEPENDS ON MARINATING THE TOMATOES LONG ENOUGH TO MARRY THE FLAVOURS. YOU CAN SERVE IT SEVERAL DAYS LATER – IT JUST GETS BETTER AND BETTER. FANCY A WARM SOUP? THEN HEAT THE GAZPACHO AND GARNISH WITH CROÛTONS, BASIL LEAVES AND A SWIRL OF OLIVE OIL.

Asparagus with poached egg and smoked prawns

SERVES **4** AS A STARTER

SMOKED PRAWNS:
250g medium raw prawns in shell, heads on
120g oak dust or wood chips (for smoking)
150g butter
2 tsp finely chopped chervil
2 tsp finely chopped dill
2 tsp finely chopped tarragon
a drizzle of vegetable oil

ASPARAGUS AND POACHED EGGS:
4 large eggs
1 tsp white wine vinegar
sea salt and black pepper
16 asparagus spears, trimmed
olive oil

TO FINISH:
dill sprigs, to garnish
lemon wedges, to serve

1 To prepare the prawns, remove the shells and the heads, reserving these in a flat-based metal colander or steamer. Rinse the prawns, drain and refrigerate in a covered bowl.

2 Scatter the oak dust evenly in a heavy-based pan (over which the colander will sit snugly), and place over a medium heat. Fit the colander of shells into the pan. When the dust starts to smoulder and smoke, after 5–8 minutes, immediately cover the colander with a double layer of cling film, securing it firmly around the sides. The cling film will bubble up and fill with smoke. Turn the heat down and let the shells infuse with the smoke for 30 minutes. Turn off the heat and release the smoke by popping a hole in the cling film with a knife.

3 Melt the butter in a large saucepan over a low heat. Add the smoked shells, stir and cook gently for 4 minutes, then turn off the heat, cover and leave to infuse for 20 minutes. Pass through a sieve, pressing the shells to release any trapped butter. Mix about 75g of the butter with the chopped herbs (reserve any excess in the fridge for another use; to baste fish, etc).

4 To cook the smoked prawns, heat a drizzle of vegetable oil in a large frying pan over a medium-high heat. Add the prawns and sauté for 1–2 minutes until pink and just firm to the touch. Pour in the herbed butter and toss well to glaze the prawns. Immediately tip into a bowl and set aside in a warm place.

5 To poach the eggs, bring a medium, wide pan of water to the boil, with the vinegar added. Crack each egg into a separate cup. Stir the water gently to make a slow whirlpool. Drop an egg into the eye of the pool, so it seals itself in the swirling water; repeat with the other eggs. Poach gently for 1½–2 minutes, then remove with a slotted spoon; to check, press gently with your finger – the egg should feel quite soft. As soon as they are ready, place on a warm plate, season with salt and pepper and keep warm.

6 Meanwhile, toss the asparagus in olive oil to coat and season with salt. Heat a drizzle of olive oil in a large frying pan over a high heat and pan-fry the asparagus spears, rolling them around with a spatula, until lightly golden brown and blistered.

DIPPING ASPARAGUS INTO SOFT-BOILED EGGS LIKE TOAST FINGERS IS A FUN WAY TO EAT. SMOKED PRAWNS ARE WELL WORTH THE EFFORT; YOU SHOULD BE ABLE TO BUY OAK DUST OR WOOD CHIPS AT A GARDEN CENTRE.

Place a poached egg in each serving bowl and top with the prawns, spooning the herbed butter over them. Garnish with dill and serve a stack of asparagus and a lemon wedge on the side. If you're serving a meal for two, arrange in a bowl on a platter to share (as shown).

Place 4 tomato slices on each plate and drizzle
with a little vinaigrette. Place a couple of red
onion rings on top. Scatter over a few cubes of
blue cheese and some rocket and basil leaves.
Top with the caramelised onions, drizzle with
olive oil and finish with a sprinkling of sea salt.

Tomato salad with caramelised onion and blue cheese

SERVES **4** AS A STARTER
a little vegetable oil
250g onions, peeled and finely sliced
80ml balsamic vinegar
20g rocket leaves
½ bunch basil, leaves picked
3 large beef tomatoes
½ red onion, peeled and sliced into rings
200g blue cheese, cut into cubes
olive oil, to drizzle
sea salt

VINAIGRETTE:
4 tbsp olive oil
1½ tbsp white wine vinegar

1 For the vinaigrette, in a small bowl, whisk together the olive oil and wine vinegar until emulsified; set aside.

2 Place a saucepan over a low heat and add a little vegetable oil. When hot, add the sliced onions and cook gently until they are soft and caramelised, about 10–15 minutes. Add the balsamic vinegar and let bubble to reduce down until sticky, about 8 minutes, stirring often. Allow to cool. Tip into a bowl and mix in 1½ tbsp of the vinaigrette.

3 Toss the rocket and basil leaves together in a bowl and drizzle over some of the vinaigrette. Cut the tomatoes into fairly thick slices.

THIS SALAD IS ONE OF MY FAVOURITE STARTERS. I LOVE ITS SIMPLICITY AND FRESHNESS, AND THE BALSAMIC CARAMELISED ONIONS ADD A MOUTH WATERING TANG. CHOOSE BRIGHT RED TOMATOES WITH A DISTINCT FRAGRANCE.

Chilled cucumber soup with salmon tartare

SERVES **4** AS A STARTER
2 cucumbers, roughly chopped
juice of 2 lemons
2 tbsp crème fraîche, or a little more to taste
1 mint sprig
sea salt

SALMON TARTARE:
a little olive oil, for oiling
270g smoked salmon trimmings or slices
50g crème fraîche
finely grated zest of ½ lemon
1 tbsp finely chopped chives
1½ tsp finely chopped dill leaves

CUCUMBER RIBBONS:
1 cucumber
dill sprigs, to garnish
olive oil, to drizzle

1 For the salmon tartare, brush four individual 4–5cm ring moulds with olive oil and place on a lightly oiled plate. Chop the smoked salmon finely and put into a bowl with the crème fraîche, lemon zest, chives and dill. Mix well and season with salt to taste. Press the tartare firmly into the moulds, cover with cling film and refrigerate.

2 To make the cucumber ribbons, peel the cucumber; reserve the peelings for the soup. Using a mandolin or swivel vegetable peeler, cut the cucumber flesh into long ribbons. Cut out the seeds in the centre; keep these for the soup, too. Place the cucumber ribbons on a tray lined with kitchen paper to drain and chill.

3 To make the soup, set a large bowl over another large bowl of iced water to chill. Put the chopped cucumbers, reserved peelings and seeds from the ribbons, lemon juice, 2 tbsp crème fraîche and the mint into a blender and process to a purée.

4 Pass the soup through a fine sieve directly into the chilled bowl, pressing the pulp thoroughly to extract all of the juice. Season with salt to taste and add a little more crème fraîche to taste, if desired. Cover and chill.

A REFRESHING STARTER TO SERVE DURING THE SUMMER WHEN ENGLISH CUCUMBERS ARE AT THEIR BEST. IF YOU DO NOT HAVE ANY RING MOULDS, SIMPLY SHAPE THE TARTARE INTO TALL MOUNDS WITH A SPOON.

Using a metal spatula, lift a tartare mould into each bowl. Carefully unmould by gently holding the salmon tartare in place while lifting off the ring mould. Fold the cucumber ribbons in half and arrange to one side of the salmon. Garnish with dill sprigs and finish with a drizzle of olive oil and a sprinkling of sea salt. Pour the soup into a serving jug and serve alongside, for guests to help themselves.

Roasted beetroot with baby chard, goat's cheese and walnuts

SERVES **4** AS A STARTER (OR 2 AS A MAIN COURSE)

3 red beetroot, washed

sea salt

1 plain goat's cheese log, about 150g,
  without rind

40ml milk

40g baby chard leaves, or mixed baby greens,
  such as rocket or spinach

olive oil, to drizzle

WALNUT DRESSING:

100g walnuts, shelled and chopped

15g parsley leaves, finely chopped

15g chervil leaves, finely chopped

1 garlic clove, peeled and crushed

2 tbsp white wine vinegar

150ml olive oil

GLAZE:

40ml thin honey

50ml red wine vinegar

65ml olive oil

1 Preheat the oven to 200°C/Gas 6. Trim the tops and roots from the beetroot, chop the trimmings and put into a saucepan. Cut off and roughly chop a quarter of 1 beetroot; add to the pan. Sprinkle a little salt on the rest of the beetroot and wrap loosely in foil. Bake until tender when tested with a knife, 1–1½ hours. Unwrap and leave to cool.

2 In a small bowl, mix the goat's cheese with the milk, using a fork to loosen it slightly. Cover and refrigerate.

3 For the walnut dressing, toast the walnuts in a dry frying pan over a medium heat until light golden brown and starting to give off a nutty aroma. Tip into a bowl and add the herbs, garlic, wine vinegar and olive oil. Stir to combine and season with salt to taste.

4 Peel the cooled beetroot and set aside; add the skins to the other trimmings.

5 To make the glaze, pour 200–300ml water over the beetroot trimmings – just enough to cover them. Bring to the boil and simmer for 10 minutes or until the water is deep red in colour. Strain, discarding the trimmings, and return to the pan. Whisk in the honey, wine vinegar, olive oil and some salt. Simmer until reduced and thickened to a syrupy glaze, about 6–8 minutes.

6 Meanwhile, cut the beetroot into wedges. Toss into the pan and gently move them around with a spoon to coat with the glaze and heat through, about 3–5 minutes.

THIS IS A RELAXED VERSION OF ONE OF MY STAR RESTAURANT DISHES. THE SIMPLE MARRIAGE OF BEETROOT AND GOAT'S CHEESE WORKS BEAUTIFULLY AND THE GLAZE ADDS A LOVELY COMPLEXITY. IT'S A VERY EASY DISH TO PUT TOGETHER.

Place a ring of beetroot wedges on
each plate and drizzle with the glaze.
Dollop the goat's cheese in between
and spoon on the walnut dressing.
Arrange the salad leaves decoratively
and sprinkle with a few drops of olive
oil and a little sea salt.

Layer the potatoes, avocado and trout in the middle of each serving plate, making a neat pile. Place a dollop of horseradish cream on top and garnish with radish slices, dill leaves and pea shoots or salad leaves. Drizzle the plate with olive oil and finish with a sprinkle of sea salt.

Jersey Royals with avocado, smoked trout and horseradish cream

SERVES **4** AS A STARTER

4 Jersey royal potatoes, cleaned
sea salt
2 thyme sprigs
2 garlic cloves, peeled and crushed
1 tbsp white wine vinegar
3 tbsp olive oil
150g smoked rainbow trout
1 avocado
juice of ¼ lime

HORSERADISH CREAM:
1½ tbsp double cream
1 tsp horseradish sauce, or a little more to taste

GARNISH:
4–5 radishes, sliced
dill leaves
small handful of pea shoots or baby salad leaves
olive oil, to drizzle

1 For the potatoes, bring a pan of well-salted water to the boil with the thyme and garlic added. Add the potatoes and boil steadily until cooked through, about 7–9 minutes; test with a knife. Drain the potatoes and peel while still warm. Place in a bowl, cover and chill.

2 In a small bowl, whisk the wine vinegar, olive oil and a couple of pinches of salt together to make a vinaigrette. Cut the cold potatoes into 1cm thick slices, add to the dressing and toss gently to coat. Leave to marinate in the fridge for at least 30 minutes, up to an hour.

3 For the horseradish cream, lightly whip the cream in a small bowl, then fold in the horseradish sauce. Cover and chill.

4 Check the smoked trout for small bones, removing any with tweezers, then break into bite-sized pieces.

5 Halve the avocado, remove the stone and peel off the skin. Cut the flesh crossways into slices, season with salt to taste and drizzle with the lime juice.

AN ASSEMBLY OF FANTASTIC INGREDIENTS THAT'S BECOME VERY POPULAR WITH REGULAR CUSTOMERS. TROUT MAY NOT BE THE MOST EXCITING OF FISH, BUT WHEN IT IS SMOKED, IT TASTES AMAZING. NOTE THAT ADDING JERSEY ROYALS TO BOILING RATHER THAN COLD WATER HELPS TO PRESERVE THEIR FLAVOUR.

Summer cherry tomatoes with crab salad

SERVES **4** AS A STARTER

16 cherry tomatoes on the vine
sea salt
olive oil, to drizzle
170g good-quality tinned crabmeat in brine
25g shallots, peeled and very finely chopped
1½ tsp finely chopped parsley
2 hard-boiled large eggs, shelled and diced
2 tbsp mayonnaise
2 or 4 slices of sourdough bread (depending on size)
dill sprigs, to garnish

1 Cut the tomato vines to make bunches of 4 or 5 tomatoes. Bring a pan of salted water to the boil and have a bowl of iced water ready. Using a sharp knife, score a small cross on the bottom of each tomato. Blanch them on their vines for 30–45 seconds, then immediately immerse in the iced water.

2 Peel the skins back carefully towards the stem without tearing them off. Drizzle with olive oil and sprinkle with salt. Cover and chill until ready to serve.

3 Drain the crabmeat and place in a small bowl. Gently mix in the shallots, chopped parsley, hard-boiled eggs and mayonnaise, using a rubber spatula. Season with salt to taste, cover and refrigerate. Remove from the fridge about 15 minutes before serving.

4 When ready to serve, heat a griddle pan over a high heat. Lay the slices of bread on the griddle at an angle and cook for about 1 minute on each side, until scorched with lines. Cut each slice in half.

CRAB IS ONE OF MY FAVOURITE INGREDIENTS AND GOES PERFECTLY WITH SWEET SUMMER TOMATOES. THIS IS A CRACKING LITTLE STARTER OR LIGHT LUNCH DISH, WHICH YOU CAN MAKE AHEAD, GIVING YOU THE OPPORTUNITY TO RELAX AND SPEND TIME WITH YOUR GUESTS.

Pile the crab salad onto the griddled sourdough and garnish with a few sprigs of dill. Place on a board, drizzle with olive oil and sprinkle with sea salt. Arrange the vine tomatoes alongside.

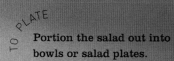

Portion the salad out into
bowls or salad plates.

Spiced green papaya and roasted peanut salad

SERVES **4** AS A STARTER

1 large green papaya (about 300g)
4 garlic cloves, peeled and finely diced
2 bird's eye chillies, finely diced
2 red chillies, deseeded and finely diced
1½ tbsp dried shrimp, roughly chopped
2½ tbsp fish sauce
juice of 2 limes
1 tbsp palm sugar (or soft brown sugar)
4 plum tomatoes, halved, deseeded and cut into strips
160g bean sprouts
bunch of coriander, leaves picked
5 tbsp peanuts, roasted and crushed
sea salt

1 Peel, halve and deseed the papaya, then shred the flesh finely.

2 Using a pestle and mortar, pound the garlic and chillies together to a paste. Add the dried shrimp and pound roughly. Add a handful of the papaya, crushing it roughly. Tip in the fish sauce, lime juice and sugar and pound together until the sugar is dissolved.

3 Transfer the pounded mixture to a large bowl, add the rest of the papaya and toss well. Add the tomatoes, bean sprouts, coriander and crushed peanuts. Toss to combine, then season with salt to taste.

I MAKE THIS THAI SALAD AT HOME A LOT – IT'S THE PERFECT DISH TO TOSS TOGETHER AND ENJOY WITH A CHILLED BEER. YOU CAN ADD SOME SHREDDED CHICKEN FOR A MORE SUBSTANTIAL SALAD IF YOU LIKE. GREEN PAPAYAS ARE AVAILABLE FROM CHINATOWN AND ASIAN FOOD STORES.

Butternut squash with ricotta and lemon honey

SERVES **4** AS A STARTER

700g butternut squash
sea salt
50g plain flour, seasoned with salt
2 eggs, beaten
70g Japanese panko breadcrumbs
vegetable oil, for deep-frying

LEMON HONEY:
60g thin honey
finely grated zest of ¾ lemon
3 tsp lemon juice

RICOTTA CHEESE:
150g ricotta cheese
about 40ml milk

GARNISH:
handful of rocket leaves
about 12 large Parmesan shavings
finely shredded zest of 1 lemon

1 Preheat the oven to 190°C/Gas 5. Cut the squash into large wedges, discarding the seeds. Place in the centre of a large piece of foil on a baking tray and season with salt. Wrap tightly and bake for about 45 minutes, until very tender. Cool slightly, then cut away the skin and roughly chop the squash into 3cm pieces.

2 Place the squash in a frying pan over a very low heat and cook gently for about 15 minutes to dry out, stirring often. The squash should break down and become pasty; do not allow it to brown. Season with salt to taste, tip into a wide dish and allow to cool. Cover and chill for about 20 minutes.

3 For the lemon honey, in a small bowl, whisk together the honey, lemon zest and juice, and 40ml water until smoothly combined. Set aside.

4 In a bowl, mix the ricotta with enough milk to give a spreadable consistency, using a fork.

5 Shape the chilled squash into 12 quenelles. To do this, dip 2 tablespoons into warm water, then pass a generous spoonful of the mixture between them, scooping and rolling the mixture as you do so to create a smooth oval. Place the quenelles on a tray lined with cling film and chill for at least 20 minutes to firm up.

6 When ready to serve, have the seasoned flour, beaten eggs and breadcrumbs ready in separate bowls. One at a time, coat each butternut quenelle in flour, then dip in the beaten eggs, and finally roll in the breadcrumbs to coat evenly.

7 Heat a 6–7 cm depth of oil in a suitable deep, heavy pan until it registers 200°C on a frying thermometer. Deep-fry the squash quenelles in batches until golden brown and crisp all over, about 2 minutes. Remove with a slotted spoon and drain on kitchen paper. Keep warm while you deep-fry the rest.

BUTTERNUT SQUASH IS A SWEET, SUCCULENT TREAT AND THESE TEMPTING PARCELS WILL IMPRESS YOUR GUESTS. USE ANY SQUASH TRIMMINGS TO MAKE A COMFORTING SOUP – COOK IN A LITTLE CHICKEN STOCK AND PURÉE WITH CREAM.

TO PLATE

Smear 2 spoonfuls of the ricotta
cheese on each plate and nestle
3 warm butternut quenelles on
top. Scatter over the rocket and
Parmesan shavings. Drizzle with
a little lemon honey and sprinkle
with lemon zest and sea salt.
Serve the rest of the lemon honey
on the side.

TO PLATE

Arrange the vegetables on serving
plates and scatter over the goat's
cheese and herbs from the marinade.
Drizzle with olive oil and a little
of the reserved marinade. Sprinkle
lightly with sea salt.

Grilled Mediterranean vegetable salad
with goat's cheese

SERVES **4** AS A STARTER (OR 2 AS A MAIN COURSE)

2 red peppers
4 garlic cloves, peeled
100ml olive oil, plus extra to drizzle
2 courgettes, trimmed
1 aubergine, trimmed
1 red onion, peeled
50ml balsamic vinegar
2 rosemary sprigs
2 thyme sprigs
2 bay leaves
110g firm goat's cheese, diced
sea salt

1 Hold each red pepper on a fork over a gas flame or place under a hot grill and turn occasionally until the skin blisters and blackens all over. Place in a bowl, cover tightly with cling film and leave to steam for 3–5 minutes. Peel off the skins, then cut the peppers in half and remove the core and seeds. Cut each half into 3 or 4 pieces and place in a deep rectangular dish.

2 Heat up a griddle pan or the grill to medium-high. Place the garlic cloves on a piece of foil, drizzle with olive oil and wrap to form a parcel. Place on one side of the griddle or under the grill (to cook alongside the vegetables).

3 Slice the courgettes and aubergine lengthways into 5mm thick strips and slice the red onion into rings. Griddle or grill the courgette, aubergine and onion slices in batches until softened and cooked through, about 3–4 minutes on each side. Add the cooked vegetable to the red peppers, laying them flat in the dish.

4 In a small bowl, mix together the balsamic vinegar, 100ml olive oil, herbs and garlic cloves. Pour this dressing over the warm vegetables and leave to marinate at room temperature for 30 minutes. Drain the vegetables, reserving the marinade.

THIS DISH IS GREAT ON A LAZY HOT SUMMER'S DAY, WHEN YOU CAN JUST PLUNK IT ON THE TABLE FOR EVERYONE TO ENJOY. IT IS REALLY IMPORTANT TO MAKE IT IN ADVANCE, SO THAT THE VEGETABLES HAVE TIME TO MARINATE IN THEIR OWN JUICES.

Pasta in mushroom sauce with poached egg and white asparagus

SERVES **4** AS A STARTER (OR 2 AS A MAIN COURSE)

12 white asparagus spears, trimmed and halved
sea salt and black pepper
2–3 tbsp olive oil, plus extra to drizzle
200g mezzi tubetti or macaroni
150g field mushrooms, cleaned and thinly sliced
250ml double cream
50ml vegetable stock
4 large eggs
1 tsp white wine vinegar

GARNISH:
35g Parmesan cheese
baby watercress sprigs

1 To cook the asparagus, bring a pot of salted water to the boil. Add the asparagus and simmer until tender, about 7 minutes. Remove with tongs and season with salt. Keep warm.

2 Add 1 tbsp olive oil to the asparagus cooking water and bring back to the boil. Add the pasta and cook until al dente, about 8 minutes. Drain and set aside.

3 Meanwhile, heat 1–2 tbsp olive oil in a medium saucepan. Add the mushrooms and sauté over a medium heat until tender, about 4 minutes. Pour in the cream and vegetable stock. Bring to the boil, then immediately take off the heat. Tip into a blender and purée until completely smooth.

4 To poach the eggs, bring a medium, wide pan of water to the boil, with the vinegar added.

Crack each egg into a separate cup. Stir the water gently to make a slow whirlpool. Drop one egg into the eye of the pool, so it seals itself in the swirling water. Repeat with the other eggs and poach gently for 1½–2 minutes, then remove with a slotted spoon; to check, press gently with your finger – the egg should feel quite soft. As soon as they are ready, place the poached eggs on a warm plate, season with salt and pepper and keep warm.

5 While the eggs are poaching, pour the mushroom purée back into the saucepan and place over a medium-low heat. Simmer for about 3–4 minutes to thicken slightly. Remove from the heat and mix in the pasta. Season with salt and pepper to taste.

6 Using a vegetable peeler, shave the Parmesan to make large, fine shavings.

THIS IS MY TAKE ON MACARONI CHEESE – A CREAMY MUSHROOM SAUCE AND PARMESAN SHAVINGS REPLACE THE USUAL CHEESE SAUCE. I SERVE IT WITH A POACHED EGG – THE CREAMY YOLK MELDS BEAUTIFULLY WITH THE EARTHY MUSHROOMS. A LOVELY VEGETARIAN DISH THAT'S ALSO GREAT FOR BRUNCH.

TO PLATE

Place a poached egg in each serving bowl and spoon the mushroom pasta alongside. Arrange the asparagus next to the eggs. Scatter with Parmesan shavings and baby watercress, and drizzle with olive oil to serve.

TO PLATE

Place 3 prawn cakes on each warm plate and scatter with the spring onions, coriander and dill. Sprinkle with salt and serve with lime wedges.

Spicy prawn cakes with a spring onion garnish

SERVES **4**

700g frozen peeled raw prawns, thawed
2 large eggs, beaten
2 spring onions, trimmed and finely chopped
2 tbsp Dijon mustard
2 tsp lemon juice
4 tsp hot chilli sauce
½ tsp sea salt
black pepper
130g Japanese panko breadcrumbs
3 tbsp olive oil

GARNISH:
4 spring onions
coriander leaves
dill leaves

TO SERVE:
lime wedges

1 Put about one-third of the raw prawns into a food processor and pulse to a smooth paste. Transfer to a large bowl.

2 Meanwhile, chop the remaining prawns into 1cm pieces. Add to the prawn paste with the beaten eggs, chopped spring onions, mustard, lemon juice, chilli sauce, salt, a grinding of pepper and 50g of the breadcrumbs. Mix well with your hands until evenly combined.

3 Shape the mixture into 12 patties, about 7cm in diameter, and coat with the remaining breadcrumbs. Place on a tray, cover and chill for 1 hour to firm up.

4 Meanwhile, prepare the garnish. Slice the green part of the spring onions on the diagonal, then slit the white part lengthways to open it out slightly. Set aside.

5 Place a large non-stick frying pan over a medium heat and add the olive oil. When hot, pan-fry the prawn cakes in 2 batches for about 4 minutes on each side until golden brown and cooked through. Drain on kitchen paper and keep warm.

AN INCREDIBLY EASY AND VERY TASTY DISH THAT YOU CAN MAKE ALL YEAR ROUND, THOUGH IT IS AT ITS BEST IN THE SPRING WHEN SPRING ONIONS ARE AT THEIR SWEETEST. SERVE WITH YOUR FAVOURITE CHILLI SAUCE ON THE SIDE.

Butternut squash soup with crayfish and lime chantilly

SERVES **4** AS A STARTER
1 butternut squash (800–900g)
3 tbsp olive oil
120g good-quality crayfish in brine, drained
about 500ml vegetable stock
50ml double cream, or to taste
30g Parmesan cheese, freshly grated
sea salt and black pepper

LIME CHANTILLY:
100ml double cream
finely grated zest of ½ lime

GARNISH:
grated zest of 1 lime
olive oil, to drizzle

1 Preheat the oven to 160°C/Gas 3. Halve, deseed and peel the squash, then cut into wedges and place on a large sheet of foil on a baking tray. Drizzle with the olive oil and wrap tightly in the foil. Roast in the oven for about 1½ hours until the squash is soft.

2 Meanwhile, for the lime chantilly, lightly whip the cream in a small bowl, then fold in the grated lime zest.

3 Let the roasted squash cool slightly and then chop roughly. Purée the squash in a blender, in batches if necessary, until completely smooth.

4 Transfer the squash purée to a large frying pan and place over a very low heat to dry out until thickened, stirring frequently with a wooden spoon. This will take about 15 minutes; don't let it brown. In the meantime, rinse the crayfish and drain well.

5 Tip the squash purée into a large saucepan, add the vegetable stock and bring to a simmer over a medium-low heat. Whisk in the cream and grated Parmesan. Season to taste and add more stock or cream to adjust the consistency if necessary. Pour the soup into a serving jug and keep warm.

INEXPENSIVE AND TASTY, CRAYFISH ARE A GOOD ALTERNATIVE TO PRAWNS AND LOBSTER. THE LIME ZEST BRIGHTENS THE WHOLE DISH AND COMPLEMENTS THE SILKY BUTTERNUT SOUP PERFECTLY.

Put a spoonful of lime chantilly into each
soup bowl and pile the crayfish on top.
Sprinkle with lime zest and add a drizzle
of olive oil. Pour the soup into the bowls
at the table.

Place a salmon fillet on each plate and top with a spoonful of pea mousse. Arrange the cucumber and crayfish around the salmon and sprinkle lightly with salt. Scatter over the watercress and drizzle with olive oil. Serve any extra pea mousse on the side.

Salmon with pea mousse and crayfish tails

SERVES **4** AS A STARTER

260g skinless salmon fillet (preferably lightly
   smoked), cut into 4 portions
600ml vegetable oil
sea salt
80g good-quality crayfish tails in brine, drained
½ cucumber

PEA MOUSSE:
1 large (or 2 small) sheet(s) of leaf gelatine
½ tsp caster sugar, plus a pinch or two
300g frozen peas
75ml double cream, lightly whipped
½ tsp lemon juice

GARNISH:
handful of watercress sprigs or pea shoots
olive oil, to drizzle

1 To cook the salmon, heat the vegetable oil in a wide, heavy-based pan and place over a very low heat until it registers 55°C on a frying thermometer. Lower the salmon fillets into the oil and poach them gently at this temperature for 6–8 minutes, adjusting the heat to keep it at 55°C as necessary. With a slotted spoon, carefully remove the salmon fillets and drain them on kitchen paper. Transfer to a plate, cover and refrigerate.

2 For the pea mousse, soften the leaf gelatine by soaking in cold water to cover. Meanwhile, bring a pan of salted water to the boil, with a pinch of sugar added. Have ready a bowl of iced water. Add the peas to the pan, bring back to the boil and blanch for 1–2 minutes. Drain, reserving 80ml of the liquid, and immediately plunge the peas into the iced water to refresh.

3 Squeeze the gelatine to remove excess water, then dissolve in the reserved hot cooking liquid. Drain the cooled peas and tip into a blender. Add the dissolved gelatine and blend to a smooth purée. Pass through a fine sieve into a bowl, pressing the pulp to extract all of the juice; you should have about 200ml.

4 Using a rubber spatula, fold the whipped cream, sugar and lemon juice into the pea purée. Season with salt and add a little more sugar, to taste, if needed. Chill to set.

5 Just before serving, rinse the crayfish tails and pat dry. Peel the cucumber, halve lengthways and deseed, then cut into batons.

6 Take the salmon out of the fridge 15 minutes before serving to bring to room temperature.

ANOTHER LOVELY DISH SHOWCASING NATURE'S VIVID COLOURS.
FOR A SHORTCUT, SIMPLY BUY READY-TO-EAT COLD SMOKED
SALMON FILLETS, OT HOT-SMOKED IF EASIER TO FIND. JUST
PORTION THE FISH AND ASSEMBLE THE DISH.

Tuna crostini with cannellini beans and marinated artichokes

SERVES **4** AS A STARTER
100g tinned tuna (in olive oil)
6 marinated artichoke hearts, halved
150g tinned cannellini beans, drained
2 tsp chopped parsley
2 tsp chopped shallots
6 sun-blushed (semi-dried) tomatoes, halved lengthways
4 slices of country bread
4 tbsp Aïoli (see page 184)
handful of rocket leaves
sea salt
olive oil, to drizzle

1 Heat up a ridged griddle pan over a medium-high heat.

2 Flake the tuna into a bowl. Add the artichoke hearts, cannellini beans, parsley, shallots and sun-blushed tomatoes, and toss together.

3 Toast the bread on the hot, dry griddle for about 2 minutes on each side until attractively marked with scorch lines.

I FIRST TASTED THIS DISH IN THE SUMMER OF 2009 AT
NEIL PERRY'S RESTAURANT IN MELBOURNE, AUSTRALIA.
I LOVED THE FLAVOURS AND TEXTURES SO MUCH THAT
I FELT I HAD TO SHARE IT WITH YOU.

Spread each slice of toast with aïoli and place on a serving plate. Pile the tuna mixture on top and scatter over the rocket leaves. Sprinkle with sea salt and add a generous drizzle of olive oil.

Arrange the mooli discs overlapping on each plate to form a crescent. Spoon the mackerel tartare into the centre of the plates. Top with a neat spoonful of avocado purée and garnish with radish julienne, coriander, dill and hogwort, if available. Sprinkle with a little pepper and add a drizzle of olive oil.

Mackerel tartare with pickled mooli and avocado purée

6 mackerel fillets, skin on (about 370g in total)
sea salt and black pepper
25g shallots, peeled and finely diced
finely grated zest of 2 lemons
1 dill sprig, finely chopped
2 tbsp capers, finely chopped
45g crème fraîche
2 tsp olive oil, plus extra to drizzle

PICKLED MOOLI:
½ mooli (Japanese radish)
2 tbsp white wine vinegar
90ml olive oil

AVOCADO PURÉE:
1 avocado
juice of ¼ lime

GARNISH:
2–3 radishes, cut into thin julienne
coriander leaves
dill sprigs
hogwort buds (optional)

1 Rinse the mackerel fillets in cold water and pat dry with kitchen paper. Sprinkle both sides generously with salt and place in a deep dish. Cover and refrigerate for 1½ hours.

2 Rinse the mackerel fillets to remove the salt, pat dry with kitchen paper and check for small bones, removing any with kitchen tweezers. Remove the skin and cut the mackerel into 5mm dice.

3 Put the diced mackerel into a bowl with the shallots, lemon zest, dill, capers, crème fraîche and olive oil. Mix gently with a rubber spatula and season with salt to taste. Cover and chill.

4 Peel the mooli and slice crossways into wafer-thin slices, with a mandolin if possible. Using a small cutter, stamp out neat 4–5cm discs from the mooli slices, 28 in total. In a small bowl, whisk together the wine vinegar and olive oil. Add the mooli discs, turning them to coat in the dressing. Cover and leave to marinate in the fridge for at least 1 hour. Drain before assembling the dish.

5 For the avocado purée, halve, stone and peel the avocado, then roughly chop the flesh. Place in a blender or small food processor with the lime juice and whiz to a smooth purée. Season with salt to taste, cover and chill.

THIS MOUTH-WATERING STARTER TASTES EVEN BETTER THAN IT LOOKS. THE TARTNESS OF THE MOOLI OFFSETS THE RICHNESS OF THE MACKEREL TO DELICIOUS EFFECT. AN EXCELLENT WAY TO USE THIS NATIVE, SUSTAINABLE FISH.

Soused mackerel with carrot, apple and chickpea salad

6 mackerel (or herring) fillets (about 50g each)

PICKLING LIQUOR:
300ml cider vinegar
300ml white wine vinegar
1 star anise pod
1 tbsp black mustard seeds
1 cinnamon stick
200g granulated or caster sugar

SALAD:
12 radishes, halved lengthways
12 baby carrots, peeled and cut in half
½ green apple
1 tsp lemon juice

HUMMUS:
400g tin chickpeas, drained
1 tbsp tahini
about 75ml olive oil
sea salt
3 tsp lemon juice, or to taste

GARNISH:
dill sprigs
black pepper
olive oil, to drizzle

1 Rinse the mackerel fillets, pat dry with kitchen paper and check for small bones, removing any with kitchen tweezers. Halve each fillet lengthways, lay in a shallow dish, cover and chill.

2 To prepare the pickling liquor, put all the ingredients into a pan and slowly bring to the boil, stirring to dissolve the sugar. Let cool to room temperature.

3 Pour about two-thirds of the cooled pickling liquor over the mackerel fillets to cover. Place the radishes and carrots in a separate bowl and pour on the remaining liquor. Cover both containers and place in the fridge. Leave to marinate for 3 hours.

4 In the meantime, make the hummus. Put the chickpeas and tahini into a blender or food processor and blitz to a purée. With the motor running, slowly add the olive oil through the funnel until you have the desired consistency. Season with salt and add lemon juice to taste.

5 Just before serving finish the salad. Core and finely slice the apple, using a mandolin if possible. Immediately sprinkle with the lemon juice to prevent discoloration. Drain the radishes and carrots and toss with the apple. Drain the mackerel fillets, too.

MARINATING RAW VEGETABLES AND FISH IS A GREAT WAY TO PRESERVE THEIR FRESHNESS NATURALLY. THE MACKEREL YOU USE MUST, OF COURSE, BE SPANKING FRESH. SURPRISINGLY, PERHAPS, HUMMUS WORKS WELL HERE AS IT COUNTERACTS THE TARTNESS OF THE DISH.

TO PLATE

Spoon some hummus onto each plate.
Lay 3 mackerel fillets on the hummus
and pile the salad on top. Garnish with
dill and finish with a grinding of pepper
and a drizzle of olive oil. Serve with
crusty bread.

TO PLATE

Arrange a few pieces of
pollock and some mussels in
each warm serving bowl with
a couple of fried bread rounds.
Spoon on the bourride and
garnish with coriander leaves.

Bourride of pollock and mussels

SERVES **4**

12–16 large mussels
600g skinless pollock fillet
1 tbsp vegetable oil
2 shallots, peeled and finely chopped
¼ red pepper, deseeded and thinly sliced
1 tbsp chopped celery
2 pinches of saffron strands
1 red bird's eye chilli, deseeded and finely chopped
finely grated zest of ½ orange
500ml chicken stock
5 tbsp Aïoli (see page 184)
sea salt and black pepper
4 slices of white bread
30g butter
coriander leaves, to garnish

1 Scrub the mussels clean under cold running water and pull away their beards. Discard any that are damaged or open and do not close when sharply tapped. Rinse the pollock fillet, pat dry with kitchen paper and cut into 5cm pieces. Set aside with the mussels.

2 Heat the oil in a large saucepan over a low heat. Add the shallots, red pepper and celery and fry gently for 5 minutes or until softened.

3 Add the saffron, chilli and orange zest and cook for a further 3 minutes. Pour in the chicken stock and bring to the boil, then reduce the heat and simmer for 3 minutes. Add the mussels, put the lid on the pan and cook for 3–4 minutes, just until the shells open. Now add the pollock pieces and warm until just cooked through.

4 Take the pan off the heat and transfer the mussels and pollock to a warm bowl, using a slotted spoon; discard any unopened mussels. Keep warm.

5 Pour the soup into a blender and blend until smooth, then with the motor running, slowly add the aïoli through the funnel. When the mixture begins to thicken, stop blending and pour back into the saucepan. Warm the bourride gently and whisk with a balloon whisk or a hand-held stick blender to make it foamy. Season to taste and keep warm.

6 Using a 4cm pastry cutter, cut 8 rounds from the bread slices. Melt the butter in a non-stick frying pan and fry the bread rounds until dark golden brown and crisp on both sides. Remove and drain on kitchen paper.

I ORDERED THIS SOUP A DECADE AGO IN A MODEST BISTRO IN MONACO – THEN RUN BY FRANCK CERRUTI – AND I'VE LOVED IT EVER SINCE. BOURRIDE IS A VARIATION OF BOUILLABAISSE, SPIKED WITH CHILLI AND ORANGE ZEST, THICKENED WITH AÏOLI AND SERVED WITH FRIED BREAD.

TO PLATE

Arrange 4 tomato slices on each plate or shallow serving bowl. Pile the squid salad on top and scatter over a few parsley leaves.

Marinated squid with cucumber and tomatoes

SERVES **4**

450g squid, cleaned
sea salt and black pepper
2 tbsp olive oil, plus extra for frying
1 tbsp red wine vinegar
½ cucumber, trimmed
4 medium tomatoes
1 tbsp finely chopped parsley
1 tbsp finely chopped chives
½ red onion, peeled and finely chopped
10 cherry tomatoes, halved
flat-leaf parsley leaves, to garnish

1 Cut the squid pouches into 1.5cm rings and the tentacles into 4cm pieces. Season with salt and pepper. Place a large frying pan over a high heat and add a little olive oil. When hot, sauté the squid for 1–2 minutes until just firm and beginning to curl. Remove from the pan and drain on kitchen paper.

2 Now place the squid in a bowl and toss with the 2 tbsp olive oil and the wine vinegar. Cover and chill for 2 hours.

3 Peel the cucumber and halve lengthways, then scrape out the seeds with a teaspoon and discard. Cut into batons, about 3cm in length. Sprinkle with salt and leave to drain in a colander for 15 minutes.

4 Rinse the cucumber under cold running water and pat dry with kitchen paper. Chill for 20 minutes.

5 Slice the medium tomatoes fairly thickly and lay on a plate. Season with salt and pepper, cover and chill for 20 minutes.

6 Add the chopped herbs, onion, cucumber and cherry tomatoes to the squid. Toss to combine, then taste and adjust the seasoning.

AN EASY GRILLED SALAD THAT CRIES OUT FRESHNESS. THIS IS THE TYPE OF FOOD I LOVE TO EAT – SIMPLE, FULL OF FLAVOUR AND NATURALLY BEAUTIFUL.

Plaice and artichoke barigoule

SERVES **4**

4 plaice fillets (180–200g each), skinned
sea salt
1 carrot, peeled and cut in half
6 tbsp olive oil
2 shallots, peeled and cut into julienne
1 garlic clove, peeled and roughly chopped
300g marinated baby artichoke hearts, rinsed and drained
2 thyme sprigs
2 pinches of saffron strands
finely grated zest and juice of ½ lemon
500ml chicken stock
coriander sprigs, to garnish

1 Rinse the plaice fillets, pat dry with kitchen paper and check for small bones, removing any with kitchen tweezers. Season with salt, cover and chill.

2 Cut 4 or 5 even lengthways grooves in the carrot pieces (to give a decorative effect when sliced). Now cut into wafer-thin slices, using a mandolin if possible, and set aside.

3 Place a heavy-based wide pan over a medium-high heat and add 4 tbsp olive oil. Add the shallots and garlic and sauté for 3–4 minutes until just softened.

4 Add the artichoke hearts, carrot slices, thyme sprigs and saffron to the pan. Cook for 2 minutes, then add the lemon zest and juice. Pour in the chicken stock and bring to a simmer. Cook until the carrots are just tender, about 4–5 minutes. Turn off the heat and keep the barigoule warm.

5 Place a non-stick frying pan over a medium-high heat and add the remaining 2 tbsp olive oil. When hot, add the plaice fillets and fry for about 2 minutes on each side, depending on thickness, until golden brown on the surface and just cooked through.

I DISCOVERED BARIGOULE WHEN I WAS WORKING FOR MARCO PIERRE WHITE. THE SHARPNESS OF THE VINEGAR AND THE EARTHINESS OF THE ARTICHOKES IS A WINNING COMBINATION. USE GIANT PLAICE (AS PICTURED) IF YOU CAN FIND IT. AVAILABLE FROM SEPTEMBER THROUGH DECEMBER, IT HAS A RICH FLAVOUR AND BUTTERY TEXTURE – LIKE HALIBUT.

Lay a plaice fillet on each warm plate and spoon the barigoule over and around the fish. Garnish with coriander and serve any extra barigoule on the side.

Divide the hot plaice fillets between individual plates and arrange the pak choi and lime wedges alongside. Serve the chilli dipping sauce in a bowl on the side. If you're serving a meal for two, arrange the pak choi, plaice and lime wedges on a platter to share (as shown).

Deep-fried plaice and pak choi with chilli dipping sauce

SERVES **4**

400g plaice fillets, skinned
sea salt
70g plain flour, seasoned with salt
1 large egg, beaten
70g Japanese panko breadcrumbs
4 heads baby pak choi
2 tbsp olive oil
vegetable oil, for deep-frying

CHILLI DIPPING SAUCE:
2 tbsp vegetable oil
2 garlic cloves, peeled and finely sliced
20g fresh root ginger, peeled and finely sliced
100g granulated or caster sugar
200ml rice vinegar
3 red chillies, deseeded and finely chopped

TO SERVE:
lime wedges

1 First, prepare the chilli dipping sauce. Place a frying pan over a high heat and add the vegetable oil. When hot, add the garlic and fry briefly until just light golden brown. Remove with a slotted spoon and drain on kitchen paper, allowing it to crisp up. Repeat the process with the ginger. Allow to cool, then roughly chop the garlic and ginger slices.

2 Combine the sugar, rice vinegar and chillies in a large heavy-based pan over a medium heat and slowly bring to the boil, stirring frequently to dissolve the sugar. Lower the heat and simmer for about 3–5 minutes until the sauce has reduced by half. Remove from the heat and mix in the garlic and ginger. Whisk in 50ml warm water or more, to achieve the desired consistency. Pour into a shallow serving dish and set aside.

3 Rinse the plaice fillets, pat dry with kitchen paper and check for small bones, removing any with kitchen tweezers. Slice lengthways into smaller pieces, 8 in total, and season both sides with salt. Have ready the flour, beaten egg and breadcrumbs in separate shallow dishes.

4 Quarter the pak choi lengthways, rinse well and pat dry with kitchen paper. Drizzle with olive oil and sprinkle lightly with salt.

5 When ready to serve, heat the oil for deep-frying in a deep, heavy pan until it registers 190°C on a frying thermometer. Meanwhile, dredge each piece of plaice in flour, then dip in beaten egg and finally coat with breadcrumbs. Deep-fry the coated plaice fillets in the hot oil for 2–3 minutes until light golden brown. Drain on kitchen paper.

THIS DISH IS A FUNNY HOMAGE TO FISH AND CHIPS, WITH A LITTLE SWEET AND SPICY SAUCE I CAME ACROSS IN ASIA. THE SAUCE GOES WITH ALMOST ANYTHING – IF YOU HAVE ANY LEFT OVER, TRY SERVING IT WITH CHICKEN OR JACKET POTATO.

Sea bream with tomato and corn salsa

SERVES **4**

4 sea bream fillets (about 160g each), skin on
olive oil, for brushing and drizzling
sea salt and black pepper

SALSA:
1 corn on-the-cob, kernels stripped
3 tomatoes, halved and deseeded
1 avocado, halved, peeled and stoned
½ cucumber, trimmed
½ yellow pepper, cored and deseeded

½ red onion, peeled
1 spring onion, trimmed
1 garlic clove, peeled
1 green chilli, halved and deseeded
juice of 1 lime
4 tbsp olive oil
2 tsp chopped coriander leaves

GARNISH:
rocket leaves

1 Rinse the sea bream fillets, pat dry with kitchen paper and check for small bones, removing any with kitchen tweezers. Lightly score the skin side of the fish fillets, using a sharp knife. Cover and chill.

2 For the salsa, simmer the corn kernels in a pan of boiling water until tender, about 6–8 minutes. Drain, refresh under cold running water and drain well. Tip the corn kernels into a large bowl.

3 Dice the tomatoes, avocado, cucumber and yellow pepper; finely dice the red onion, spring onion, garlic and chilli. Add these ingredients to the corn with the lime juice, olive oil and coriander. Toss to combine and season well with salt and pepper. Cover and chill for 1 hour.

4 Brush the fish fillets with olive oil and season well. Heat a griddle pan or the grill to medium-high. When hot, add the fish, skin side down. Cook for 2–3 minutes on each side, depending on thickness, until just cooked through.

OVER THE PAST COUPLE OF YEARS, I HAVE BECOME A HUGE FAN OF MEXICAN FOOD. I LOVE THE CONTRASTING SWEET/ SOUR FLAVOURS, ASSORTED TEXTURES AND COLD/HOT COMBINATIONS THAT CHARACTERISE THE DISHES. THIS MARRIAGE OF CHILLED CHOPPED VEGETABLES SPIKED WITH CHILLI AND HOT GRIDDLED FISH HAS A MEXICAN FEEL ABOUT IT.

Place a bream fillet on each warm plate, spoon on some of the chilled salsa, top with a pile of rocket and add a drizzle of olive oil. If you're serving a meal for two, arrange the 2 bream fillets on a platter to share and top with the salsa and rocket (as shown). Serve the extra salsa on the side.

Place a fish fillet on each warm
plate and spoon on a portion of
patatas bravas.

Pan-fried fish with patatas bravas

SERVES **4**

4 plaice or other white fish fillets
(180–200g each), skinned
2 tbsp olive oil

PATATAS BRAVAS:
1 head of garlic
4 tbsp olive oil
sea salt
800g tinned tomatoes
1 tsp dried chilli flakes
2 bay leaves

½ tsp dried thyme
½ tsp dried oregano
1 onion, peeled, halved and thinly sliced
1 red pepper, halved, cored, deseeded and
thinly sliced
100ml dry white wine
1–2 tbsp caster sugar, to taste
1½ tsp paprika
3 large Maris Piper or similar potatoes
vegetable oil, for deep-frying
½ tsp garlic granules
3 coriander sprigs, leaves picked

1 Rinse the fish fillets, pat dry with kitchen paper and check for small bones, removing any with kitchen tweezers. Cover and chill.

2 For the patatas bravas, break apart the garlic and set aside half of the cloves in their skins. Peel and finely chop the rest. Heat 2 tbsp olive oil in a large frying pan over a medium-low heat. Add the chopped garlic with a pinch of salt and cook for 1 minute until just softened. Stir in the tomatoes and cook for about 7 minutes, to reduce slightly. Add the chilli flakes, bay leaves, thyme and oregano. Cook, stirring often, until reduced and thickened, about 6–7 minutes. Tip into a bowl; set aside.

3 Wipe the frying pan clean and place over a medium-high heat. Add 2 tbsp olive oil and sauté the onion and red pepper until softened, about 4 minutes. Add the white wine and let bubble until reduced down to almost nothing. Add the tomato and garlic mixture, sugar and 1 tsp paprika. Simmer for a few minutes to

reduce further. Season with salt to taste and a little more sugar if you think it is needed.

4 Cut the potatoes lengthways into wedges and pat dry with kitchen paper. Heat the oil for deep-frying in a suitable pan to 160°C. Deep-fry the potatoes and unpeeled garlic cloves in batches for 8–10 minutes until cooked through and slightly coloured. Drain on kitchen paper.

5 Raise the oil temperature to 180°C. Fry the potatoes again, for 5 minutes or until golden brown and crisp. Drain on kitchen paper, then toss with the remaining ½ tsp paprika, garlic granules and a few pinches of salt. Add the potatoes and garlic cloves to the tomato sauce and toss well. Stir in the coriander leaves.

6 Place a large frying pan over a medium-high heat and add 2 tbsp olive oil. When hot, add the fish, skin side down, and cook for 2–3 minutes on each side, depending on thickness, until golden brown and just cooked through.

PATATAS BRAVAS HAS BEEN A FIRM FAVOURITE EVER SINCE I LIVED IN SPAIN. THIS IS MY TAKE ON THE SPANISH CLASSIC, WHICH YOU'LL FIND EASY TO DO AT HOME. MEATY GIANT PLAICE IS IDEAL HERE IF AVAILABLE; OTHERWISE USE STANDARD PLAICE OR OTHER FISH FILLETS.

Baked pollock with ginger, soy, lime and sticky rice

SERVES **4**

200g short-grain white (sushi) rice
2 large pollock fillets (about 400g each), skinned
sea salt and black pepper
2 tsp grated fresh root ginger
2 garlic cloves, peeled and finely chopped
juice of 1 orange
1 green chilli, thinly sliced
2 tbsp soy sauce
2 tbsp mirin (Japanese rice wine)
2 coriander sprigs, leaves picked and chopped
25g baby spinach
1 lime, cut in half

GARNISH:
1 green chilli, thinly sliced on the diagonal
handful of coriander leaves
few dill sprigs (or extra coriander leaves)

1 Preheat the oven to 180°C/Gas 4. Wash the rice in cold water 3 times to remove any starch residue, then soak it in cold water to cover for 45 minutes.

2 Rinse the fish fillets, pat dry with kitchen paper and check for small bones, removing any with kitchen tweezers. Season both sides with salt and pepper. Cut 2 large sheets of foil and place a pollock fillet in the centre of each. Scrunch the foil around each fish gently, making an oval bowl shape, then lift onto a baking tray.

3 Drain the rice and cook it according to the packet instructions (bearing in mind that the fish parcels will take about 20 minutes to assemble and cook).

4 In a small bowl, whisk together the ginger, garlic, orange juice, chilli, soy sauce, mirin and coriander. Pour the mixture evenly over each fish fillet. Crimp the edges of the foil together over the fish to seal tightly and place in the oven. Bake for 15–17 minutes, then remove from the oven and leave to stand, still sealed in the foil, for 2 minutes; the fish will continue to cook in the residual heat.

5 Open the foil carefully and poke some baby spinach leaves under and around each fish fillet. Squeeze the juice from a lime half over each fillet.

WHEN I AM TRAVELLING THROUGH ASIA, I ALWAYS TRY TO TAKE IN AS MANY DIFFERENT DISHES AS POSSIBLE – THE FLAVOUR COMBINATIONS ARE SO INSPIRING. THE IDEA FOR THIS RECIPE CAME FROM A MEAL I HAD IN A BANGKOK RESTAURANT. COOKING SIMPLE WHITE FISH IN A SEALED FOIL BAG WITH ASIAN SPICES IS A GREAT WAY TO FLAVOUR IT.

TO PLATE

Simply place the fish parcels on a board and serve straight from the foil.
Scatter chilli slices and coriander leaves on top of the fish. Serve the sticky
rice garnished with a few herbs in a bowl on the side.

Place each pollock fillet on an elegant serving board or plate. Grind over some pepper and add a dollop of aïoli. Arrange the tomatoes, quail's eggs, olives, fennel and potatoes in little piles around the board and stack the beans on top of the potatoes. Drizzle decoratively with olive oil.

Poached pollock with Niçoise salad and aïoli

SERVES **4**
600g skinned pollock fillet
1.2 litres fish stock
2 thyme sprigs
1 large garlic clove, peeled and crushed
2 tsp lemon juice
sea salt and black pepper

AÏOLI:
5 garlic cloves (skin on)
20ml double cream
pinch of saffron strands
50g Mayonnaise (see page 184)

NIÇOISE SALAD:
250g cherry tomatoes, halved
olive oil, to drizzle
2 garlic cloves, peeled and crushed
4 thyme sprigs, leaves picked
200g green beans, trimmed
12 Charlotte potatoes, scrubbed clean
6 quail's eggs
1 medium fennel bulb, trimmed
4 dill sprigs, leaves picked
16–20 marinated black olives, stoned and halved

1 Cut the pollock into 4 portions. Pour the fish stock into a pan, add the thyme, garlic and lemon juice and place over a high heat. When it is just about to boil, add the fish fillets and reduce the heat. Poach gently for about 7–9 minutes until cooked through. Carefully remove from the liquid, drain on kitchen paper and allow to cool; reserve the poaching liquid.

2 For the aïoli, bring the poaching liquid back to the boil. Add the unpeeled garlic cloves and cook for 4–6 minutes until very soft. Lift out with a slotted spoon and peel off the skins. Using a pestle and mortar, pound the garlic, gradually adding the cream to make a smooth paste. Turn into a bowl and fold in the saffron and mayonnaise. Chill for 30 minutes to infuse, then season with salt to taste.

3 Preheat the oven to 130°C/Gas ½. Drizzle the cherry tomatoes with olive oil, and toss with the garlic, thyme and some salt. Place flat side up on a baking tray and roast in the oven for 20–25 minutes until starting to wrinkle.

4 Bring the poaching liquid back up to the boil and blanch the green beans for about 3 minutes until al dente. Remove with a slotted spoon and immediately plunge into a bowl of iced water to refresh. Drain and toss with a little olive oil and salt. Cover and refrigerate.

5 Add the potatoes to the poaching liquid, bring back to the boil and cook for 7–9 minutes until tender when pierced with a knife. Remove with a slotted spoon and peel off the skins while still hot. Allow to cool, then cut in half and season with salt.

6 Add the quail's eggs to a pan of boiling water and cook for 2½ minutes to soft boil. Place immediately in a bowl of iced water to cool quickly, then drain and halve lengthways.

7 Slice the fennel into fine wedges and immerse in a bowl of iced water to crisp up and remove the bitterness, about 10 minutes. Drain, then dress with olive oil and salt, and toss with the dill. Chill.

THIS CLASSIC DISH IS AT ITS BEST IN THE SUMMER WHEN PRODUCE IS FRESH AND VIBRANT. IT HAS A LOVELY CASUAL FEEL, BUT LOOKS IMPRESSIVE ENOUGH TO SERVE AT A DINNER PARTY.

Sea bream with pak choi and tomato and ginger chutney

SERVES **4**

4 sea bream fillets (about 150g each), skin on
sea salt and black pepper
3 tbsp olive oil, plus extra to drizzle

TO SERVE:
2 heads pak choi
lime wedges

CHUTNEY:
40g brown sugar
1 tbsp honey
40ml rice vinegar
1 cinnamon stick
4 medium tomatoes, chopped
1 tbsp chopped fresh root ginger
½ tsp cracked coriander seeds
1 tbsp chopped mint leaves

1 Rinse the fish fillets, pat dry with kitchen paper and check for small bones, removing any with kitchen tweezers. Season both sides with salt and pepper, cover and chill.

2 To make the chutney, put the brown sugar, honey, rice vinegar and cinnamon stick into a saucepan and stir over a medium-high heat until the sugar is dissolved. Reduce the heat and add the tomatoes, ginger and coriander. Cook slowly over a low heat, stirring from time to time, until the mixture has thickened to a chutney consistency, about 30 minutes. Discard the cinnamon stick and stir in the chopped mint. Season with salt and pepper to taste. Keep warm.

3 While the chutney is cooking, prepare the pak choi by breaking the heads apart and trimming the base of each leaf. Wash the leaves and pat dry with kitchen paper. Heat 1 tbsp olive oil in a non-stick pan and sauté the pak choi until just wilted. Season with salt and keep warm.

4 Heat 2 tbsp olive oil in a large non-stick frying pan over a medium-high heat. Lay the fish fillets in the pan, skin side down, and cook for 2 minutes or until the edges are golden, then turn and cook on the other side for a minute or two until just cooked through. Remove to a warm plate and season with salt.

SEA BREAM IS ONE OF MY FAVOURITE FISH AND IT IS NOT EXPENSIVE. LIKE SEA BASS, IT WORKS WELL WITH ALL MANNER OF FLAVOURS. THE CHUTNEY IS BEST MADE IN SUMMER WHEN TOMATOES ARE AT THEIR SWEETEST.

Place a bream fillet in the centre of each warm plate. Add a couple of spoonfuls of chutney. Arrange the pak choi and lime wedges on top and drizzle the plate with a circle of olive oil.

TO PLATE

Place each mackerel parcel on a platter and spoon
the extra filling on top. Garnish with rocket and
a few basil leaves and drizzle lightly with olive oil.
Cut each parcel in two to serve.

Stuffed mackerel with Mediterranean flavours

SERVES **4**

4 mackerel fillets, skin on
sea salt and black pepper
1 red pepper
2 small courgettes, trimmed
6 tbsp olive oil, plus extra to drizzle
5 garlic cloves, peeled and finely chopped
1 thyme sprig
1 bay leaf
4 marinated artichoke hearts, rinsed, drained
   and halved
3 cherry tomatoes, halved
12 black olives, halved and pitted
1 basil sprig, leaves picked

GARNISH:
handful of rocket leaves
few basil leaves

1 Preheat the oven to 180°C/Gas 4. Rinse the mackerel fillets, pat dry with kitchen paper and check for small bones, removing any with kitchen tweezers. Season each side with salt and pepper, cover and chill.

2 Hold the red pepper on a fork over a gas flame or place under a hot grill and turn occasionally until the skin blisters and blackens all over. Place the pepper in a bowl, cover tightly with cling film and leave to steam for 3–5 minutes. Peel off the skin, then cut the pepper in half and remove the core and seeds. Cut each half into 4 pieces.

3 Slice the courgettes lengthways into fine ribbons, with a mandolin if possible. Set aside.

4 Heat a large, wide non-stick pan, add 2 tbsp olive oil and sauté the garlic until just softened. Toss in the thyme and bay leaf and cook for 1–2 minutes, then add the courgette ribbons and sauté for 3 minutes until just softened. Add the artichokes, cherry tomatoes and olives and cook for another 3–4 minutes until the tomatoes are just beginning to wilt. Remove from the heat and let cool slightly.

5 Lay 2 mackerel fillets side by side on a foil-lined baking tray, placing four 15cm lengths of kitchen string crossways at equal intervals under each fillet. Layer some of the courgette ribbons, pepper pieces, tomatoes, garlic cloves, artichokes, olives and basil leaves on top, but do not overstuff the fish; spoon any extra filling around the fillets.

6 Lay the other mackerel fillets on top to sandwich the filling and tie securely; cut off excess string. Season with salt and drizzle 2 tbsp olive oil over each parcel. Bake in the oven for about 10 minutes until cooked through, basting the fish with the cooking juices halfway through.

I'M VERY FOND OF MACKEREL. IT MAY BE ONE OF THE CHEAPEST FISH YOU CAN BUY BUT IT HAS A GREAT FLAVOUR – PROVIDED YOU EAT IT VERY FRESH. I'VE USED A CLASSIC COMBINATION OF MEDITERRANEAN VEGETABLES HERE, BUT FEEL FREE TO VARY IT.

Grilled salmon steak with ginger chilli glaze and sticky rice

SERVES **4**

300g short-grain white (sushi) rice
4 salmon steaks (about 300g each)
sea salt and black pepper
vegetable oil, for brushing

CHILLI MARINADE:
4 red chillies, deseeded and thinly sliced
3 tsp grated fresh root ginger
400ml orange juice
200ml light soy sauce
130ml white wine vinegar
140g granulated or caster sugar

GARNISH:
coriander leaves
olive oil, to drizzle

1 Rinse the rice a few times in cold water to remove excess starch, then soak in cold water to cover for 45 minutes. Rinse the salmon steaks and pat dry with kitchen paper. Season both sides with salt and pepper, then cover and refrigerate.

2 To make the chilli marinade, put the chillies, ginger, orange juice, soy sauce, wine vinegar and sugar into a saucepan. Bring to the boil, stirring to dissolve the sugar, and let bubble for 10–12 minutes to reduce down and thicken, stirring often. Season with a little salt. Pour into a wide bowl and leave to cool completely.

3 Lay the salmon steaks in a fairly deep baking dish and pour the cooled chilli marinade over them. Cover and leave to marinate in the fridge for an hour.

4 Drain the rice and cook according to the packet instructions until tender.

5 Meanwhile, lift the salmon steaks out of the marinade with tongs onto a plate. Pour the marinade into a saucepan and simmer over a medium heat until reduced and thickened, about 5 minutes. Keep warm.

6 Brush the grill rack with vegetable oil and heat to medium-high. Once hot, grill the salmon steaks for about 5 minutes on each side, depending on thickness, until cooked to your liking.

SALMON STEAKS ARE, OF COURSE, WIDELY AVAILABLE, BUT RARELY COOKED IN AN ADVENTUROUS WAY. THIS RECIPE IS FOR THOSE WHO APPRECIATE SOUTHEAST ASIAN FLAVOURS AND LIKE THINGS WITH A BIT OF HEAT.

Place each salmon steak on a plate and spoon over some of the chilli glaze. Garnish with coriander leaves and drizzle with a little olive oil. Serve the sticky rice in a bowl on the side.

Haddock with warm leek, potato and apple salad

4 haddock fillets (about 180g each), skinned
sea salt and black pepper
3 tbsp finely chopped shallots
1 garlic clove, peeled and finely chopped
1½ tsp chopped parsley
3 tbsp white wine
2 tbsp white wine vinegar
3 tbsp olive oil, plus extra for frying
6 medium fingerling or other small new potatoes
1 leek, trimmed and cut in half crossways
1 Granny Smith apple, halved
1 tsp lemon juice

1 Rinse the haddock fillets, pat dry with kitchen paper and check for small bones, removing any with kitchen tweezers. Season both sides of the fillets with salt, place on a plate, cover and chill.

2 In a bowl, whisk together the shallots, garlic, parsley, white wine, wine vinegar and olive oil to make a vinaigrette. Season with salt and pepper to taste and set aside.

3 Put the potatoes into a saucepan, add cold water to cover, salt well and bring to the boil. Lower the heat and simmer for 8–10 minutes or until tender right through when pierced with a knife. Drain and leave until cool enough to handle, then peel and halve crossways. Place in a bowl, season and keep warm.

4 Meanwhile, add the leek to a separate pan of boiling salted water and cook until tender, about 10 minutes. Drain, pat dry and slice into 1cm thick rounds, taking care not to break them apart. Add to the bowl with the potatoes.

5 Cut 12 wafer-thin slices from the apple, using a mandolin if possible, and toss with the lemon juice. Cut out the core from each slice. Add the apple slices to the potatoes and leeks. Pour the vinaigrette over the salad and toss gently. Keep warm.

6 Heat a drizzle of olive oil in a large non-stick frying pan. Add the haddock fillets and fry for 2–3 minutes on each side, depending on thickness, until cooked through and lightly browned. Remove to a warm plate.

THERE IS SOMETHING VERY COMFORTING ABOUT THE MARRIAGE OF POTATO AND LEEK, PAIRED HERE WITH PAN-FRIED HADDOCK AND APPLE FOR A SIMPLE DISH THAT CAN BE SERVED AT ANY TIME OF THE YEAR.

Place a haddock fillet on each warm plate. Spoon the leek, potato and apple salad on top and drizzle over some of the vinaigrette to finish.

Divide the warm salad between
warm plates, arranging the squid
decoratively on top of the tomatoes
and beans. Garnish with mint leaves.

Roasted squid with minty broad beans

SERVES **4**

400g squid, cleaned
1 tbsp sweet paprika
1 tbsp ground cumin
7 tbsp olive oil
sea salt and black pepper
320g shelled broad beans
6 plum tomatoes, deseeded and diced
2 parsley sprigs, leaves picked and
  roughly chopped
1 garlic clove, peeled and finely chopped

1 tbsp finely chopped shallots
juice of 1 lemon
1 mint sprig, leaves picked and finely shredded,
  plus extra leaves to garnish
1 tbsp sherry vinegar

1 Cut the squid pouches into 2cm thick rings and place in a large bowl with the tentacles, paprika, cumin and 4 tbsp olive oil. Toss to mix, cover and leave to marinate in the fridge for about 2 hours.

2 Bring a pan of salted water to the boil. Add the broad beans and cook for about 3 minutes until tender. Drain, refresh in iced water, then drain and remove the tough outer skins. Put the broad beans into a large bowl and mix with the diced tomatoes.

3 Place a large frying pan over a high heat and add the remaining 3 tbsp olive oil. Cook the squid in batches for about 2 minutes until tender and lightly golden. Return all of the squid to the pan and reduce the heat to medium. Mix in the chopped parsley, garlic and shallots. Add the lemon juice and sauté for another 2 minutes.

4 Take the pan off the heat and toss in the broad beans and tomatoes. Add the shredded mint and sherry vinegar, toss well and season with salt and pepper to taste.

I AM A BIG FAN OF SQUID AND CUTTLEFISH AS I LOVE THEIR TEXTURE AND UNIQUE FLAVOUR. MINT AND BROAD BEANS HAVE A NATURAL AFFINITY AND WORK WELL WITH PAN-FRIED SQUID IN THIS COLOURFUL DISH.

Sea bream with fennel salad and orange dressing

SERVES **4**

4 sea bream fillets (about 160g each), skin on

sea salt and black pepper

100ml olive oil, plus extra to drizzle

3 oranges (blood oranges when in season)

1 fennel bulb, trimmed, leafy tops reserved (or use
  dill sprigs if the fennel is ready trimmed)

½ red onion

3 tbsp white wine vinegar, plus an extra splash

75g stoned marinated black olives, quartered lengthways

3 tbsp vegetable oil

1 Rinse the fish fillets, pat dry with kitchen paper and check for small bones, removing any with kitchen tweezers. Score 4 or 5 shallow cuts on the skin side of each. Season and drizzle with olive oil. Cover and refrigerate.

2 Segment 1 orange by slicing off the peel and pith and cutting between the membranes to release the segments; do this over a small pan to catch the juice. Put the segments into a small boilable plastic bag and seal. Squeeze the juice from the pithy membrane into the pan.

3 Grate the zest from the other 2 oranges into a bowl. Squeeze the juice and add to the pan. Let bubble over a medium heat to reduce by two-thirds. Pour over the zest, cool and chill.

4 Chop a few of the fennel tops (or dill), saving the rest for garnish. Slice the fennel bulb and onion finely into ribbons, using a mandolin if possible. Immediately plunge into a bowl of iced water. Leave for 10 minutes until crisp.

5 To make the sauce, immerse the bag of orange segments in a small pan of boiling water to the count of 10. Place the bag on your worktop and gently press apart the segments with your fingers, making orange pearls. Add these to the reduced juice and zest with the wine vinegar, 100ml olive oil and half the chopped fennel tops (or dill). Mix gently.

6 Drain the fennel and onion slices, pat dry and place in a bowl. Set aside 12 olive pieces for garnish. Add the rest of the olives to the bowl with the remaining chopped fennel tops (or dill), a generous drizzle of olive oil, a splash of wine vinegar and a generous pinch of salt. Toss together.

7 Heat the vegetable oil in a frying pan over a medium-high heat. Pan-fry the fish fillets, skin side down first, for 1–2 minutes on each side until the edges are golden. Remove to a warm plate and season with salt.

IF EVER A DISH SPEAKS FRESHNESS, THIS IS IT. I LOVE ITS SIMPLE ELEGANCE AND VIBRANT COLOURS. BLOOD ORANGE ADDS REAL ZING TO THE DRESSING AND A SALAD OF RED ONION AND FENNEL LENDS A CRISP, REFRESHING ELEMENT. YOU CAN SERVE THE SALAD ON THE SIDE RATHER THAN ON TOP OF THE FISH IF YOU PREFER.

TO PLATE

Drizzle orange sauce around each warm plate and place a bream fillet, skin side up, in the centre. Drizzle a little sauce over the fish. Pile the fennel salad on top and finish with the feathery fennel or dill. Scatter the reserved olive pieces around the plate and serve, with the extra sauce on the side.

TO PLATE

Arrange the gurnard and the olive
and artichoke salad on warm plates
and garnish with parsley leaves.

Gurnard with olives and artichokes

SERVES **4**

700g skinned gurnard fillet
2–3 globe artichokes
1 lemon, halved
sea salt
1 rosemary sprig
2 garlic cloves, peeled and chopped
1 bay leaf
2 thyme sprigs
7 tbsp olive oil
4 tbsp chopped shallots
50g pitted black olives, chopped
2 tbsp chopped flat-leaf parsley, plus extra leaves to garnish

1 Rinse the fish in cold water, pat dry with kitchen paper and check for small bones, removing any with kitchen tweezers. Cut into 4 portions (or 8 smaller pieces), cover and chill.

2 Now prepare the artichokes one at a time. Have ready a bowl of cold water with the juice of one lemon half added. Trim away the artichoke leaves down to the heart (save the soft leaves to nibble on later), scrape out the hairy choke and immerse the artichoke heart in the lemon water to prevent discoloration.

3 Bring a pan of salted water to the boil and add the rosemary, garlic, bay leaf and thyme. Squeeze in the juice from the other lemon half, add both spent lemon halves and bring to the boil. Drain the artichokes and add to the pan. Lower the heat to a simmer and cook until tender, 15–20 minutes. Remove the artichoke hearts with a slotted spoon and leave to cool. Cut into wedges, season with salt and set aside.

4 Place a large non-stick frying pan over a medium heat and drizzle in 3 tbsp olive oil. When hot, add the shallots and olives and cook for 3 minutes or until the shallots are just softened. Tip into a bowl and toss in the chopped parsley.

5 Heat another 2 tbsp olive oil in the same frying pan, add the artichoke hearts and sauté over a medium heat until tinged golden brown at the edges, 4–5 minutes. Place in the bowl with the shallots and olives and toss together. Keep warm.

6 Wipe the frying pan out with kitchen paper, place over a high heat and drizzle in the remaining 2 tbsp olive oil. When it is hot, add the gurnard pieces to the pan and fry for 1–2 minutes on each side, depending on thickness. Season lightly with salt.

AS DEPLETING FISHING STOCKS CONTINUE TO BE A CONCERN, SUSTAINABLE SPECIES LIKE GURNARD COME INTO THEIR OWN. HERE'S A FANTASTIC WAY OF SERVING THIS UNDERUSED FISH, WHICH WAS ONCE CONSIDERED ONLY FIT FOR THE SOUP POT.

Salted cod with winter cabbage, bacon and beer sauce

SERVES **4**

4 skinned cod fillets (about 120g each)
15g sea salt
½ pointed Hispi cabbage
about 4 tbsp olive oil, plus extra to drizzle
2 shallots, peeled and sliced
3 thyme sprigs, leaves picked
2 garlic cloves, peeled and finely chopped
250ml bitter (English beer)
600ml chicken stock

100ml double cream
1 tsp lemon juice
175g thick-cut bacon, cut into 5cm long batons
120g baby onions, peeled
40g butter
2 tbsp dark brown sugar
6 bay leaves, split in half lengthways, to garnish

1 Rinse the cod fillets, pat dry with kitchen paper and check for small bones, removing any with kitchen tweezers. Lay on a tray and sprinkle with the salt, coating both sides evenly. Wrap in cling film and refrigerate for 4–6 hours. Rinse the cod in cold water to remove the salt and pat dry with kitchen paper. Cover and chill.

2 Trim the cabbage, cutting out the core, then slice into 6cm thick strips. Blanch in a pan of boiling salted water for 2–3 minutes until just tender. Immediately drain and immerse in a bowl of iced water. Drain and set aside.

3 To make the beer sauce, heat a drizzle of olive oil in a large saucepan over a medium heat and sauté the shallots for a few minutes to soften. Add the thyme leaves and garlic and cook for another 3–4 minutes. Pour in the beer and let bubble to reduce down to almost nothing, 4–5 minutes. Pour in 500ml of the chicken stock, increase the heat to medium-high and reduce by half, about 8 minutes. Add the cream and simmer gently for about 5 minutes to reduce and thicken, then stir in the lemon juice.

4 While the sauce is reducing, cook the bacon and onions. Place a wide pan over a medium heat and add a drizzle of olive oil. When hot, fry the bacon until just crisp and golden, then remove and drain on kitchen paper.

5 Add the butter, sugar, remaining chicken stock and baby onions to the oil remaining in the pan and cook, turning frequently, until the onions are tender and caramelised, 5–6 minutes. Return the bacon to the pan and toss well. Keep warm.

6 When the sauce is ready, add the blanched cabbage and turn to coat and warm through. Set aside; keep warm.

7 Heat a non-stick frying pan over a medium-high heat and add 3 tbsp olive oil. When hot, fry the bay leaves until just crisp, about 1 minute. Remove and drain on kitchen paper.

8 Now add the cod fillets to the frying pan and fry for about 4 minutes each side, depending on thickness, until cooked through and golden around the edges.

THIS IS A NOD TOWARDS MY TIME IN ALSACE. THE GUTSY
COMBINATION OF BEER, BACON AND CABBAGE IS DELICIOUS
AND IT COMPLEMENTS SALTED COD PERFECTLY.

Divide the cabbage leaves between warm plates. Lay a cod fillet on top and scatter the bacon and shallots on and around the fish. Spoon over some of the beer sauce, drizzle the plate with olive oil and garnish with the crisp bay leaves. Serve the rest of the sauce in a jug.

Drizzle a little sardine sauce on
each platter and lay a slice of
toast in the middle. Top with
the tomato salad, followed by
the sardines, bacon and basil.
Finish with a drizzle of sardine
sauce and a little olive oil.

Grilled sardines on toast with bacon, basil and tomato

SERVES **4**

8 butterflied sardine fillets (filleted and opened out flat)

a bunch of basil, leaves picked, stalks reserved

400g cherry tomatoes, about 35-40, halved

2 tbsp finely diced red onion

4 tbsp sherry vinegar

120ml olive oil, plus extra to drizzle

1½ lemons, in halves ready for squeezing

sea salt and black pepper

vegetable oil, for frying

4 rashers of streaky bacon

120g tin sardines in tomato sauce

4 slices of thick country bread (ciabatta or sourdough)

1 garlic clove, peeled and halved

1 Check the sardine fillets for bones, cover and refrigerate. Set aside some of the basil leaves for garnish and put the rest into a bowl with half of the cherry tomatoes.

2 Add the onion, sherry vinegar, olive oil and the juice of ½ lemon to the tomatoes. Toss gently and season with salt. Cover and leave to marinate in the fridge for at least 30 minutes.

3 Meanwhile, heat a little vegetable oil in a small wide pan and fry the bacon rashers until crisp. Remove and drain on kitchen paper, trim to neaten if you like, and set aside.

4 Into the same pan, tip the tinned sardines in tomato sauce, basil stalks and remaining cherry tomatoes. Stir and let simmer over a medium heat for 10 minutes or until the tomatoes are cooked, stirring often. Remove from the heat and stir in the juice of ½ lemon. Transfer to a blender and purée until smooth, then press through a sieve into a bowl. Season.

5 Heat up a griddle or grill. Char-grill or toast the bread until golden brown, and scorched if using a griddle. Drizzle with olive oil and rub with the cut garlic clove.

6 Heat a good splash of vegetable oil in a large frying pan. Pan-fry the sardine fillets, skin side down first, for 1–2 minutes on each side until cooked. Season with a little salt and add a squeeze of lemon.

AS A CHILD I ATE MORE TINNED SARDINES ON TOAST THAN I CARE TO REMEMBER. THIS SOPHISTICATED VERSION – FEATURING FRESH SARDINES, TOMATOES AND BASIL – IS ALTOGETHER DIFFERENT.

Place a swordfish steak on
each warm plate. Garnish with
watercress and pecorino shavings
and add a drizzle of olive oil.
Serve with lime wedges.

Moroccan grilled swordfish with watercress and pecorino

SERVES **4**

4 skinned swordfish steaks (about 125g each)
sea salt and black pepper

MARINADE:

1½ tbsp cumin seeds
1½ tbsp coriander seeds
1 tsp turmeric
1 tbsp harissa
100ml olive oil
1 tbsp chopped coriander leaves
2 garlic cloves, peeled and finely chopped

GARNISH:

few handfuls of baby watercress sprigs
pecorino cheese shavings
olive oil, to drizzle

TO SERVE:

lime wedges

1 Rinse the swordfish streaks, pat dry with kitchen paper and season both sides with salt. Place in a dish, cover and chill.

2 Meanwhile, make the marinade. Toast the cumin and coriander seeds in a dry pan over a medium heat for about 1 minute until fragrant. Tip into a large bowl and let cool, then add the turmeric, harissa, olive oil, chopped coriander and garlic and toss to mix.

3 Rub the marinade over the fish steaks, re-cover and leave to marinate in the fridge for 8–12 hours, or overnight.

4 To cook the fish, heat up a griddle or the grill to medium-high. Shake off any excess marinade, then season the swordfish steaks with salt and pepper. Cook on the hot griddle or grill for 4–5 minutes each side, depending on thickness, until just cooked through.

SWORDFISH IS OFTEN OVERLOOKED, BUT IT IS A GOOD, MEATY FISH THAT READILY TAKES ON OTHER FLAVOURS. HERE, I'M USING A MIX OF SPICES. THE ADDITION OF PECORINO, ALTHOUGH UNUSUAL, LENDS A TOUCH OF CREAMINESS AND MELLOWS THE SPICY MARINADE.

Country pâté with pickles and English mustard

MAKES ABOUT **12** SLICES

250g Parma ham slices

500g minced pork

250g chicken livers, trimmed

125g streaky bacon, derinded

250g pork back fat

8g garlic, peeled and finely chopped

3 rosemary sprigs, leaves picked and finely chopped

3 thyme sprigs, leaves picked and finely chopped

¼ tsp ground cloves

¼ tsp ground mace

15g salt, or to taste

125g Japanese panko breadcrumbs

50g pistachio nuts

TO SERVE:

1 Little Gem lettuce, leaves separated

20 cornichon pickles, sliced lengthways in half

4 tbsp English mustard

olive oil, to drizzle

8 slices of country bread, grilled

1 Preheat the oven to 150°C/Gas 2. Line a 1.5 litre terrine mould or loaf tin with baking parchment. Now line the bottom and sides with Parma ham, reserving 4 slices to cover the top.

2 Put the minced pork into a large bowl. Chop the livers and bacon into 2cm pieces; cut the pork fat into 1cm pieces. Add these meats to the pork along with the garlic, herbs, spices, salt, breadcrumbs and pistachios. Mix together well, using your hands.

3 Spoon the pâté mixture into the mould and press down well to exclude any air gaps, taking care to avoid dislodging the Parma ham. Cover with the remaining Parma ham and lay a sheet of baking parchment on top. Wrap the entire terrine twice in cling film (to seal in the flavours and keep the pâté moist).

4 Stand the terrine in a small roasting tin and pour in enough warm water to come about two-thirds of the way up the side of the mould. Cook in the oven for about 1 hour, until a cooking thermometer inserted into the centre indicates that the core temperature has reached 68°C.

5 Place the terrine on a wire rack and let cool to room temperature. Now place a plate on top, weight down and chill for at least 1 hour.

6 When ready to serve, invert the pâté onto a board to unmould and remove the cling film and lining paper. Cut 4 generous slices and allow to come to room temperature. Re-wrap the rest of the terrine, refrigerate and eat within 4 or 5 days.

THIS PÂTÉ IS ONE OF THE FIRST I LEARNED TO MAKE. I LOVE THE INTEGRITY OF ITS FLAVOURS, WHICH RESPECT ITS SOUTHWEST FRANCE ORIGINS. IT ISN'T PRACTICAL TO MAKE A SMALLER TERRINE, BUT IT KEEPS WELL IN THE FRIDGE AND IS IDEAL FOR LUNCH OVER THE NEXT FEW DAYS.

Place a slice of pâté on each plate with a pile of lettuce leaves. Add a spoonful of pickles and a dollop of mustard. Drizzle with olive oil and serve with the warm grilled bread.

TO PLATE Serve the paella straight from the pan
or divide between warm plates.

Paella of chicken, squid and chorizo

SERVES **4**

4 chicken thighs (bone in)
sea salt and black pepper
200g squid, cleaned
4 tbsp olive oil
50g chorizo, sliced into 1cm rounds
¾ tsp paprika
pinch of saffron strands
½ tsp dried oregano
pinch of dried chilli flakes

1 tomato, diced
½ onion, peeled and diced
2 garlic cloves, peeled and finely chopped
250g paella rice
750ml fish stock
finely grated zest of ½ orange
3 tbsp vegetable oil
1½ tbsp chopped parsley

1 Preheat the oven to 150°C/Gas 2 and put a baking tray in to heat up. Rinse the chicken thighs and trim off any fat. Season with salt. Slice the squid pouches into 1cm rings, place in a bowl with the tentacles, cover and chill.

2 Place a paella pan or shallow casserole dish over a medium heat and add 2 tbsp olive oil. When hot, add the chorizo and fry, stirring, until just coloured. Add the paprika, saffron, oregano, chilli flakes, tomato, onion and garlic. Stir and cook for about 3–4 minutes until the onion and garlic are softened, then tip in the rice. Cook for about 3–4 minutes, stirring.

3 Pour in the fish stock and stir in the orange zest and ½ tsp salt. Bring to the boil, stirring occasionally. Turn the heat down to a low simmer. Cook, uncovered, for about 15 minutes without stirring until the rice is tender, while retaining a bite.

4 While the paella is simmering, cook the chicken. Place a frying pan over a medium-high heat and add the vegetable oil. Pat the chicken thighs dry with kitchen paper and sear in the hot pan for 4–5 minutes on each side to colour and crisp the skin. Transfer to the hot baking tray and place in the oven for about 5 minutes to cook through.

5 To cook the squid, heat the remaining 2 tbsp olive oil in a large frying pan over a high heat. Fry the squid, in batches if necessary, for 1½–2 minutes until lightly coloured. Season with salt and pepper.

6 Just before serving toss two-thirds of the squid and chopped parsley through the paella and check the seasoning. Top with the chicken thighs and scatter over the remaining parsley and squid.

ONE OF THE FIRST DISHES I COOKED AT EL BULLI WAS A TRADITIONAL CATALAN PAELLA OF SQUID AND RABBIT. I HAVE CHANGED THE RABBIT TO CHICKEN, BUT OTHERWISE THE RECIPE IS SIMILAR, AND A FITTING HOMAGE TO MY TIME AT EL BULLI. YOU CAN EASILY HALVE THE QUANTITIES TO SERVE TWO.

Grilled chicken with tamarind and herb salad

SERVES **4**

4 chicken breasts (preferably supremes,
  with the wing bone attached)
vegetable oil, for brushing
sea salt

MARINADE:
30g tamarind paste
8g coriander seeds
50g palm sugar (or brown sugar)
2 tbsp soy sauce
2½ tbsp oyster sauce
2½ tsp salt
1½ tsp ground white pepper
1 tsp ground black pepper

HERB SALAD:
50g mixed fresh herbs (coriander, mint and basil)
3 spring onions, trimmed
2 red chillies, deseeded and finely diced

TO SERVE:
lime wedges

1 For the marinade, dissolve the tamarind paste in 140ml warm water, removing any seeds. Toast the coriander seeds in a dry frying pan over a medium-high heat until golden brown, about 1–2 minutes. Tip the seeds into a mortar and crush with the pestle, then transfer to a deep dish and add the tamarind and all of the other ingredients. Mix well.

2 Place the chicken breasts in the marinade, turning to coat both sides. Cover and leave to marinate in the fridge overnight.

3 Lift the chicken out of the dish, reserving the marinade, and brush both sides with vegetable oil. Place on a plate and set aside. Pour the marinade into a saucepan and bring to the boil. Reduce the heat to medium low and simmer until reduced by a third and thickened to a sauce, about 5–8 minutes. Set aside.

4 To cook the chicken, heat up the grill. Once it is hot, place the chicken skin side down on the grill rack and cook for about 8–10 minutes on each side, depending on thickness, until cooked through.

5 In the meantime, prepare the salad. Strip the herb leaves from their stems and place in a bowl. Thinly slice the spring onions on the diagonal and add to the herbs with the chillies. Toss well.

I SPENT A LITTLE TIME IN VIETNAM A FEW YEARS AGO AND LOVED
THIS DISH FROM THE REX HOTEL IN SAIGON. THE SOURNESS OF
THE TAMARIND COMBINED WITH THE PUNGENT SALAD HERBS
LIFTS THE FLAVOURS TO CREATE A BEAUTIFULLY BALANCED DISH.

Cut the chicken breasts in half. Place skin side up on a plate and spoon some sauce over each piece. Pile the herb salad on top of the chicken and drizzle with more sauce. Sprinkle with sea salt and garnish with lime wedges.

TO PLATE

Arrange a bed of potato slices on each warm plate and place a duck leg on top. Spoon the mustard sauce on top, using the thyme sprigs as a garnish.

Duck confit with Jersey Royals and Dijon mustard

SERVES **4**

4 duck legs
5 Jersey Royal potatoes
sea salt
30g butter
vegetable oil, to drizzle

DRY BRINE:
2 tbsp salt
2 tsp ground black pepper
10 sage leaves, roughly chopped
8 thyme sprigs, leaves picked and chopped
4 rosemary sprigs, leaves picked and chopped
1 head of garlic, peeled and roughly chopped

CONFIT OIL:
1.5–2 litres vegetable oil
1 tbsp salt
½ head garlic, peeled and finely chopped
5 rosemary sprigs
5 thyme sprigs

MUSTARD SAUCE:
7 tbsp olive oil
2 tbsp finely chopped shallots
1 garlic clove, peeled and thinly sliced
5 thyme sprigs
2 tbsp white wine vinegar
1 tsp chopped parsley
2 tbsp wholegrain Dijon mustard

1 Wash the duck legs, pat dry with kitchen paper and place in a deep dish. In a small bowl, mix together the ingredients for the dry brine. Rub the mixture all over the duck legs, cover with cling film and chill overnight.

2 The next day, preheat the oven to 90°C/Gas ¼. Put the duck legs and dry brine into a deep heavy-based cooking pot. For the confit oil, mix 1.5 litres vegetable oil with the salt, garlic and herbs. Pour over the duck legs, making sure they are fully immersed; top up with more oil if necessary. Place in the oven for 2½–3 hours until the duck is cooked through and very tender, but not falling off the bone, turning the legs halfway through cooking. Lift out the duck legs onto a warm plate.

3 Meanwhile, make the mustard sauce. Heat 1 tbsp olive oil in a small frying pan and cook the shallots and garlic over a low heat until softened. Add the thyme sprigs and sauté until the leaves are crisp. Whisk in the remaining olive oil, wine vinegar, parsley and mustard. Set aside; keep warm.

4 To cook the potatoes, bring a saucepan of well-salted water to the boil. Add the potatoes and boil steadily until cooked through, about 7–9 minutes; test with a knife. Drain the potatoes and peel while still warm. Once cooled, cut into 5mm thick slices and season with salt.

5 When ready to serve, heat a drizzle of vegetable oil in a large non-stick frying pan. Add the duck legs, skin side down, and fry over a medium-high heat for about 3 minutes until the skin is crisp. Turn and fry for another 2–3 minutes. Remove from the heat and let rest in a warm place for 5 minutes. Meanwhile, heat the butter in a non-stick frying pan over a medium heat and fry the potato slices until golden.

DUCK IS CONSIDERED A RELATIVELY EXPENSIVE MEAT, BUT THE LEGS ARE CHEAP – AND DELICIOUS WHEN PROPERLY COOKED. CONFIT IS A TECHNIQUE THAT CAN BE APPLIED TO MANY CHEAPER CUTS OF MEATS.

Lamb steaks with pomegranate, avocado and Arabic bread

SERVES **4**

2 lamb leg steaks (about 400g each), bone in
sea salt and black pepper
vegetable oil, for oiling the pan
handful of coriander leaves (optional)
2 Arabic breads, or 4 pitta breads, warmed

COUSCOUS SALAD:
250g couscous
1 tbsp ground cumin
grated zest and juice of 1 lemon
100ml olive oil
50g parsley leaves, finely chopped

AVOCADO SALAD:
2 ripe large avocados
juice of 1 lime
1 red chilli, deseeded and finely chopped
1 garlic clove, peeled and crushed
10g mint leaves, finely chopped
10g coriander leaves, finely chopped

POMEGRANATE SALAD:
1 large pomegranate, seeds extracted,
  all pith removed
25ml white wine vinegar
75ml olive oil
½ medium onion, peeled and finely diced
5g mint leaves, finely chopped
5g parsley leaves, finely chopped

1 First, make the couscous salad. Put the couscous into a bowl and pour on 350ml boiling water. Cover and leave to stand for 10 minutes or until softened and the water is absorbed. Add the cumin, lemon zest and juice, olive oil, parsley and salt to taste. Mix gently, cover and keep warm.

2 For the avocado salad, halve, stone and peel the avocados and cut into 1cm dice. Toss with the rest of the ingredients in a bowl. Season with salt and pepper, cover and chill.

3 For the pomegranate salad, press half of the pomegranate seeds in a fine sieve set over a small pan with a spoon to extract the juice; you should have about 70ml. Place over a high heat and let bubble to reduce by half. Tip into a bowl, add the rest of the pomegranate seeds and the other ingredients. Toss to mix.

4 Season the lamb steaks on both sides with salt and pepper. Heat up a barbecue, griddle pan or frying pan. Oil the pan if using one. Cook the steaks for about 4 minutes on each side for medium rare, depending on thickness.

THIS UNUSUAL RECIPE IS A TRIBUTE TO MY YEARS SPENT IN THE MIDDLE EAST. IT'S
A CRACKING DISH TO MAKE FOR FRIENDS, PERFECT TO EAT WHILE WATCHING TV,
OR TO SERVE AS A MAIN COURSE FOR A MORE FORMAL DINNER PARTY.

Serve the lamb, couscous, pomegranate and avocado salads
on a board, scattered with coriander and accompanied by
warm Arabic breads wrapped in a napkin. Slice the lamb
into strips at the table. To eat, split the breads open and
stuff with a few slices of lamb and a spoonful of each salad.

Place a generous spoonful of carrot purée on each warm
plate and drag the bottom of the spoon through it to make
a circle. Lay a piece of beef on the purée and top with
a bouquet garni bundle and a small spoonful of grainy
mustard. Spoon the sauce over the meat and around the
plate.

Pork belly with minestrone and poached egg

SERVES **4**

600g skinned boneless pork belly

4 tbsp vegetable oil

1 onion, peeled and diced

1 bay leaf

1 thyme sprig

1 rosemary sprig

about 1.5 litres dark chicken stock

75g dried spaghetti, broken into short lengths

1 large carrot, peeled and diced

1 large courgette, trimmed and diced

1½ celery sticks, trimmed and diced

sea salt and black pepper

4 large eggs

1 tsp white wine vinegar

flat-leaf parsley leaves, to garnish

1 Cut the pork belly into 2 or 3 large pieces (so it will fit inside a large cooking pot) and remove any excess fat. Place a large cooking pot over a high heat and add a drizzle of vegetable oil. When hot, add the pork belly and sear on all sides, colouring it evenly. Remove to a large plate and set aside.

2 Reduce the heat to medium and add the onion, bay leaf, thyme and rosemary to the pot. Cook until the onion is softened, about 5 minutes. Pour in the chicken stock and bring to a simmer. Return the pork to the pot, making sure it is fully submerged; if necessary, top up with more stock. Simmer over a low heat for about 1½ hours until the pork is very tender. Let cool in the liquor.

3 Once cooled, lift out the pork belly onto a tray, reserving the braising liquor. Place another tray on top of the pork and weight down to press the meat. Refrigerate for at least 3 hours.

4 Strain the liquor through a fine sieve and pour two-thirds into a saucepan for the minestrone broth (freeze the rest for another dish). Bring to the boil, then add the spaghetti and cook until almost tender. Add the carrot, courgette and celery and simmer until just softened, about 3–4 minutes. Remove from the heat, taste for seasoning and keep warm.

5 Just before serving, cut the pressed pork into portions. Heat a non-stick frying pan with a drizzle of vegetable oil. When hot, pan-fry the pork until browned, about 3 minutes each side.

6 Meanwhile, poach the eggs. Bring a medium, wide pan of water to the boil, with the vinegar added. Crack each egg into a cup. Stir the water gently to make a slow whirlpool. Drop one egg into the eye of the pool, so it seals itself in the swirling water. Repeat with the other eggs and poach gently for 1½–2 minutes, then remove with a slotted spoon; to check press gently with your finger, the yolk should feel soft. As soon as they are ready, place on a warm plate; keep warm.

MY FIRST ENCOUNTER WITH MINESTRONE SOUP INVOLVED POURING A POWDER OUT OF A PACKET INTO A BOWL AND ADDING HOT WATER. I AM GLAD TO SAY MY PALATE IS A BIT MORE REFINED THESE DAYS. IT IS VERY SATISFYING TO MAKE THIS SOUP FROM SCRATCH.

Place a portion of pork in each warm
serving bowl and top with a poached
egg. Spoon in the minestrone,
season with pepper and scatter
over a few parsley leaves.

Divide the chorizo and bean stew
between warm plates. Top each serving
with a confit chicken leg and garnish
with the roasted garlic and herbs.

Confit chicken legs with chorizo bean stew and roasted garlic

SERVES **4**

4 chicken legs, about 220g each
30g butter, for cooking

DRY BRINE:

2 tbsp salt
2 tsp ground black pepper
10 sage leaves, roughly chopped
8 thyme sprigs, leaves picked and chopped
4 rosemary sprigs, leaves picked and chopped
1 head of garlic, peeled and roughly chopped

CONFIT OIL:

1.5–2 litres vegetable oil
1 tbsp salt
½ head garlic, peeled and finely chopped
5 each rosemary and thyme sprigs

CHORIZO AND BEAN STEW:

1 tbsp vegetable oil
100g chorizo sausage, cut into 5mm dice
100ml chicken stock
100ml double cream
220g tinned butter beans, drained
3 thyme sprigs, leaves picked
sea salt

ROASTED GARLIC:

1 head of garlic
8 thyme sprigs
8 sage leaves
5 tbsp olive oil

1 Wash the chicken legs, pat dry with kitchen paper and place in a deep dish. In a bowl, mix together the ingredients for the dry brine. Rub over the legs, making sure they are coated all over. Cover with cling film and chill overnight.

2 The next day, preheat the oven to 90°C/Gas ¼. Put the chicken legs and dry brine into a deep heavy-based cooking pot. For the confit oil, mix 1.5 litres oil with the salt, garlic and herbs. Pour over the chicken, making sure it is fully immersed; top up with more oil if necessary. Cook in the oven for 2–2½ hours, turning the legs after an hour, until the chicken is cooked through and very tender, but not falling off the bone. Lift out the chicken legs onto a plate.

3 For the stew, heat the oil in a heavy-based pan and fry the chorizo until lightly browned. Remove with a slotted spoon and drain on kitchen paper. Add the stock and cream to the pan, stir and bring to the boil. Lower the heat and simmer to reduce by half. Add the chorizo and beans and simmer for 10–15 minutes until the liquor has thickened. Take off the heat, add the thyme and season with salt.

4 For the roasted garlic, heat the oven to 180°C/Gas 4. Break apart but don't peel the garlic cloves. Place in the centre of a piece of foil, top with the herbs and drizzle with the olive oil. Wrap in the foil and roast for 30–45 minutes until the skins are crisp and the flesh is soft.

5 Just before serving, heat a little confit oil in a large frying pan over a high heat. Put the chicken legs in the pan, skin side down, and cook for 2–3 minutes. Turn the chicken legs and add the butter to the pan. As it melts, spoon over the chicken to crisp the skin. After 2–3 minutes, take off the heat and let rest in a warm place for a few minutes.

CHICKEN LEGS ARE OFTEN OVERLOOKED IN FAVOUR OF BREASTS, BUT COOKED IN THIS WAY, THE DARK LEG MEAT IS RICH AND TASTY. YOU CAN LEAVE OUT THE BEAN STEW AND JUST SERVE THE CONFIT LEGS WITH A LEAFY SALAD IF YOU LIKE.

Place a lamb steak on each warm plate and arrange a few squash wedges on top. Spoon over the pine nut sauce and garnish with rosemary leaves.

Lamb steaks with butternut squash, pecorino and pine nuts

SERVES **4**

4 lamb steaks (about 220g each)
sea salt
1 small butternut squash (500–600g), halved and deseeded
olive oil, to drizzle
20g pecorino cheese, grated
25g pine nuts
20g butter
150ml lamb stock
1 tbsp chopped parsley
finely grated zest of ½ lemon
rosemary leaves, to garnish

1 Trim the lamb steaks of any excess fat, season with salt and set aside.

2 Preheat the oven to 180°C/Gas 4. Cut the butternut squash lengthways into wedges. Heat a large frying pan, add a drizzle of olive oil and sear the squash wedges on both sides until golden brown. Transfer to a roasting tray and bake in the oven for about 20 minutes until soft.

3 While the squash is cooking, scatter the pine nuts on a baking tray and toast in the oven for 3–4 minutes until golden. Tip onto a board and chop roughly; set aside.

4 Meanwhile, place a large non-stick frying pan over a medium-high heat and add a drizzle of olive oil and the butter. When hot, pan-fry the lamb steaks for about 3–4 minutes on each side, according to thickness, until well browned but still pink inside.

5 Sprinkle half of the pecorino over the squash and return to the oven for 3 minutes until the cheese is melted.

6 When the lamb steaks are cooked, transfer them to a warm plate and set aside to rest in a warm place while you make the sauce.

7 Pour the lamb stock into the hot frying pan and let bubble until reduced by one-third. Remove from the heat and stir in the chopped parsley, remaining pecorino, lemon zest and pine nuts.

THIS DISH OF MEATY LAMB STEAKS WITH ROASTED BUTTERNUT SQUASH AND A RUSTIC SAUCE HAS A LOVELY AUTUMNAL FEEL. THE RICH INTENSE FLAVOUR OF BUTTERNUT MARRIES PERFECTLY WITH THE PECORINO AND PINE NUTS.

Roasted chicken with Tuscan bread salad

SERVES **4**

4 chicken breasts, skin on (ideally supremes,
 with the wing bone attached)
2 red peppers
2 tbsp olive oil, plus extra to drizzle
sea salt and black pepper
4 plum tomatoes
1 tsp sherry vinegar
1–2 tbsp vegetable oil
4 tbsp butter
1 garlic clove, peeled and thinly sliced
3 basil sprigs, leaves picked

CROÛTONS:
3 thick slices of a day-old sourdough loaf,
 or ciabatta
2 garlic cloves, peeled and halved
olive oil, to drizzle

1 First, prepare the croûtons. Preheat the oven to 150°C/Gas 2. Toast the bread in the oven for 10 minutes or until lightly coloured. Rub the cut garlic over both sides of the bread. Cut into 5cm cubes, drizzle with olive oil and sprinkle with salt. Return to the oven for 5 minutes or until golden brown and crisp. Set aside. Turn the oven up to 180°C/Gas 4.

2 Set the chicken aside at room temperature. Hold each pepper on a fork over a gas flame or place under a hot grill and turn occasionally until the skin blisters and blackens all over. Place in a bowl, cover tightly with cling film and leave to steam for 3–5 minutes. Peel off the skins, then halve the peppers and remove the core and seeds. Cut each half into 3 or 4 pieces, drizzle with olive oil and season with salt.

3 Score a little cross on the bottom of each tomato. Blanch the tomatoes in a pan of boiling salted water for 30–40 seconds, then remove and plunge into a bowl of iced water. Take out and peel off the skins. Quarter 2 tomatoes and scrape out the pulp and seeds into a food

processor, leaving tomato petals. Halve these lengthways; set aside. Roughly chop the rest of the tomatoes, add to the processor and whiz for 45 seconds. Strain through a sieve into a bowl, pressing the pulp to extract all of the juice.

4 Whisk the tomato juice with the sherry vinegar, 2 tbsp olive oil and a pinch of salt to make a tomato vinaigrette.

5 Season the chicken with salt and pepper. Heat the vegetable oil in a frying pan over a medium-high heat. When hot, cook the chicken breasts, skin side down, for 4–5 minutes, then turn them and add the butter. Once melted, spoon the butter over the chicken to glaze and crisp the skin. Cook for another 4–5 minutes.

6 Transfer the chicken to a baking tray and finish cooking in the oven for 3–5 minutes, depending on thickness. Leave to rest in a warm place for 10 minutes. Meanwhile, put the tomato petals, pepper pieces, sliced garlic, basil leaves and croûtons into a bowl. Drizzle with the tomato vinaigrette and toss to coat.

AN OLD ITALIAN FAVOURITE – SUCCULENT ROASTED CHICKEN WITH A SALAD OF PLUM TOMATOES, SWEET PEPPERS, FRAGRANT BASIL AND IRRESISTIBLE GARLIC CROÛTONS MAKES A MOST SATISFYING MEAL.

TO PLATE

Cut each chicken breast in half and place on warm plates, stacked up against each other. Arrange the salad on top and drizzle with the tomato vinaigrette and olive oil.

Place a pork chop in the centre of each warm plate. Arrange the
apple, black pudding and potato slices overlapping alternately
on top. Spoon a small dollop of apple purée onto the other side.
Garnish with the crisp thyme and drizzle the plate with the sauce.

Pork chops with black pudding and apple

SERVES **4**

4 pork chops (about 190g each)
1 tsp sugar
2 tsp lemon juice
1 Granny Smith apple
1 large red-skinned potato, scrubbed
sea salt
70g black pudding
1 tbsp olive oil
1–2 tbsp vegetable oil
60g butter
1 shallot, peeled and finely chopped

5 thyme sprigs, leaves picked
1 garlic clove, peeled and finely chopped
500ml cider
500ml veal or light beef stock
250ml chicken stock
1 tbsp wholegrain mustard

TO SERVE:
thyme sprigs, to garnish
Apple purée (see page 183)

1 Preheat the oven to 170°C/Gas 3. Set the pork chops aside at room temperature.

2 Whisk the sugar and lemon juice together in a bowl. Peel the apple and cut into 5mm thick slices. Using a 4cm pastry cutter, cut out 12 rounds. Add to the lemon juice, turn to coat and leave to marinate for at least 20 minutes. (Use the trimmings for the apple purée.)

3 Cut the potato into 5mm thick slices. Add to a pan of boiling salted water and cook until just tender, about 3–4 minutes. Drain and cool on a wire rack, then transfer to a board. Using a 4cm pastry cutter, cut out 12 rounds.

4 Cut the black pudding into 5mm thick slices. Heat the olive oil in a frying pan and fry the black pudding slices until crisp. Remove and drain on kitchen paper, then cut out twelve 4cm rounds; keep warm.

5 Season the chops with salt. Heat a large heavy-based frying pan over a high heat and add a little vegetable oil. When hot, brown the chops (two at a time, if necessary) for

3–4 minutes on each side. Add the butter and, once melted, spoon over the chops to glaze them. Transfer to a baking tray and finish cooking in the oven, 3–5 minutes depending on thickness. Set aside to rest in a warm place.

6 Add the shallot to the pan and cook gently for 3–4 minutes to soften. Add the thyme leaves and garlic and cook for 2 minutes. Increase the heat to medium and pour in the cider, stirring to deglaze the pan. Let bubble until reduced down to almost nothing. Add the veal stock, bring to a simmer and reduce by half. Do the same with the chicken stock. Strain the sauce through a fine sieve and return to the pan. Whisk in the mustard and reduce until thickened, about 5 minutes.

7 Meanwhile, for the garnish, heat a little vegetable oil in a frying pan over a high heat and fry the thyme sprigs for 1–2 minutes until the leaves are glossy and crisp. Remove and drain on kitchen paper.

8 Fry the potato discs in the pan until golden, drain on kitchen paper and season with salt.

THE WOW FACTOR OF THIS DISH IS IN THE PRESENTATION – A BIT CHEFFY PERHAPS, BUT SO EASY – ALL YOU NEED IS A PASTRY CUTTER AND A FEW MINUTES. THE FLAVOUR COMBINATION ORIGINATES FROM THE NORTH, WHERE I GREW UP.

Confit duck legs with orange, ginger and watercress

SERVES **4**

4 duck legs
vegetable oil, to drizzle

DRY BRINE:
2 tbsp salt
2 tsp ground black pepper
10 sage leaves, roughly chopped
8 thyme sprigs, leaves picked and chopped
4 rosemary sprigs, leaves picked and chopped
1 head of garlic, peeled and roughly chopped

CONFIT OIL:
1.5–2 litres vegetable oil
1 tbsp salt
½ head of garlic, peeled and finely chopped
5 each rosemary and thyme sprigs

ORANGE DISCS:
2 Seville oranges (or use another sharp variety)
10g fresh root ginger, peeled
50g granulated or caster sugar

ORANGE SAUCE:
1 shallot, peeled and diced
1 garlic clove, peeled and finely chopped
200ml orange juice
20g caster sugar
500ml chicken stock
sea salt and black pepper

TO FINISH:
olive oil, to drizzle
baby watercress sprigs

1 Wash the duck legs, pat dry with kitchen paper and place in a deep dish. Mix together the ingredients for the dry brine and rub all over the duck legs. Cover and chill overnight.

2 The next day, preheat the oven to 90°C/Gas ¼. Put the duck legs and brine in a heavy-based cooking pot. For the confit oil, mix 1.5 litres oil with the salt, garlic and herbs. Pour over the duck legs, making sure they are fully immersed; top up with more oil if necessary. Place in the oven for 2½–3 hours, turning the legs halfway, until the duck is cooked through and very tender, but not falling off the bone. Lift out the duck legs onto a warm plate.

3 Meanwhile, prepare the orange discs. Halve 1 orange, wrap the halves separately and place in the freezer for an hour or until semi-frozen. Cut 12 wafer-thin slices, using a mandolin if possible, and place in a bowl. Squeeze the juice from the other orange and reserve.

4 Finely slice the ginger, ideally on a mandolin and place in a small saucepan with 50ml water, the sugar and orange juice. Slowly bring to the boil, stirring to dissolve the sugar. Pour over the orange slices and leave to cool; the slices will lightly poach in the residual heat.

5 When ready to serve, heat a little vegetable oil in a large non-stick frying pan. Add the duck legs, skin side down, and fry over a medium-high heat for 3 minutes or until the skin is crisp. Turn and fry for another 2–3 minutes. Remove to a warm place and rest for 5 minutes.

6 Meanwhile, make the sauce. Pour off excess fat from the pan, then add the shallot and garlic and cook until softened. Add the orange juice, stirring to deglaze. Add the sugar, stir to dissolve, then simmer to reduce right down. Pour in the chicken stock and reduce until shiny and thickened to a sauce consistency. Strain through a fine sieve and season to taste.

DUCK À L'ORANGE IS OFTEN OVERLY SWEET, BUT I THINK THIS VERSION HAS THE RIGHT BALANCE OF SWEET/SHARP FLAVOURS – ESPECIALLY IF BITTER SEVILLE ORANGES ARE USED.

Arrange 3 orange discs on each warm plate, shaking off any excess moisture, and place a duck leg on top. Lay another orange disc on the duck leg and garnish with a few of the ginger slices. Spoon some sauce over the meat and around the plate and drizzle with a little olive oil. Finish with a scattering of watercress.

Braised lamb with imam bayildi and black olives

SERVES **4**

700g lamb necks, trimmed
sea salt
4 tbsp vegetable oil
½ onion, roughly chopped
½ carrot, roughly chopped
½ celery stick, roughly chopped
½ leek, roughly chopped
1 tsp tomato purée
1 garlic clove, peeled and chopped
1 thyme sprig
1 rosemary sprig
250ml white wine
500–600ml dark chicken stock
500–600ml beef stock
250g tinned tomatoes

IMAM BAYILDI:
2 aubergines
1 tbsp fine salt
1 tbsp olive oil
1 onion, peeled and thinly sliced
1 tsp ground cumin
100g sultanas
vegetable oil, for deep-frying
2 tbsp tomato ketchup
1 tbsp chopped coriander leaves

GARNISH:
50g black olives, halved and pitted
curly parsley leaves

1 Season the lamb with salt. Heat 3 tbsp vegetable oil in a large heavy-based pan and quickly sear the lamb over a high heat, turning to colour all over. Remove to a plate.

2 Fry the onion and carrot in the pan, stirring over a medium heat, until golden. Add 1 tbsp vegetable oil, the celery, leek and a little salt. Stir-fry for 4–5 minutes. Add the tomato purée, garlic and herbs and cook for 2 minutes. Add the wine and bubble until reduced right down. Pour in 500ml of each stock and bring to the boil. Stir in the tomatoes and lower the heat. Add the lamb necks to the pan, making sure they are fully submerged; top up with stock if necessary. Turn the heat to very low and cook for 1¾–2 hours until the meat is very tender.

3 Meanwhile, for the imam bayildi, cut the aubergines into 2cm dice, but do not peel. Toss with the salt, place in a colander and leave to drain and release the bitter juices for 1 hour.

4 Heat the olive oil in a saucepan and cook the onion on a low heat until soft and caramelised, about 15 minutes. Stir in the cumin and cook for another 5 minutes. Tip into a bowl. Put the sultanas in a pan, add water to cover and bring to the boil, then drain and add to the onion.

5 Rinse the aubergine cubes and pat dry. Heat the oil for deep-frying in a suitable deep, heavy pan to 115°C. Deep-fry the aubergine cubes in batches for 3–4 minutes until golden and cooked through. Drain on kitchen paper, then tip into a food processor and add the ketchup, sultanas and onion. Pulse, keeping the mixture chunky. Stir in the coriander and check the seasoning. Transfer to a bowl and keep warm.

6 When the lamb is cooked, lift out onto a warm plate and rest in a warm place. Strain the liquor, pour one-third into a pan and bubble until reduced and thickened to a sauce consistency (freeze the rest for another dish).

NECK OF LAMB IS AN UNDERUSED CUT IN THIS COUNTRY BUT IT IS SUPERB
SLOWLY BRAISED AND SERVED WITH THIS TRADITIONAL TURKISH AUBERGINE DISH.

Spoon some imam bayildi onto each warm
plate. Slice the lamb and arrange on top.
Spoon over some sauce and garnish with
olives and parsley. Serve any extra
imam bayildi on the side.

sweet

Strawberry sundae

SERVES **4**

500g strawberries, hulled
4 large (or 7 small) sheets of leaf gelatine
60g caster or granulated sugar

VANILLA CHANTILLY:
300ml double cream
½ vanilla pod, split lengthways
30g icing sugar, sifted

TO ASSEMBLE:
130g Greek yoghurt
4 scoops of Vanilla ice cream (see page 181)
4 scoops of Strawberry sorbet (see page 182)

TO FINISH:
2 strawberries, thinly sliced

1 Quarter the strawberries and set aside. For the jelly, soak the gelatine leaves in cold water to cover until softened.

2 Meanwhile, put 200ml water and the sugar into a saucepan and slowly bring to the boil, stirring occasionally to encourage the sugar to dissolve. Reduce the heat to low, add the strawberries and heat gently to soften. Once they are tender and the liquid is coloured red from their juice, remove from the heat.

3 Drain the berries in a sieve over a bowl to catch the juice, then tip them into another bowl. You should have 550ml juice: save 400ml for the jelly; pour the rest over the berries.

4 Squeeze the gelatine to remove excess water, then add to the hot strawberry juice and stir until dissolved. Cover with cling film and chill until the jelly has set, about 4 hours. Cover the strawberry compote and chill at the same time.

5 For the vanilla chantilly, whip the cream until it holds soft peaks. Scrape the vanilla seeds from the pod and add them to the cream with the icing sugar. Fold in, using a spatula. Cover and chill.

MAKE THIS SUNDAE DURING THE SUMMER USING HOME-GROWN STRAWBERRIES. AT OTHER TIMES, SUBSTITUTE SEASONAL FRUIT: GREENGAGES OR PLUMS IN THE AUTUMN; POACHED PEARS OR APPLES IN WINTER; POACHED RHUBARB IN THE SPRING.

In tall glasses, layer the sundae components in the
following order: jelly, strawberry compote, yoghurt,
vanilla chantilly, vanilla ice cream, jelly, chantilly
and strawberry sorbet. Top with a few fresh
strawberry slices and serve at once.

Arrange 5 peach slices on each plate, overlapping them to form a circle. Pile the macerated diced peaches in the centre and cover with a dollop of lemon cream. Top with candied orange zest, sprinkle with almond shavings and scatter with tiny mint leaves. Finish with a drizzle of vanilla syrup.

Macerated peaches with whipped lemon cream

SERVES **4**
6 tbsp thin honey
6 lemon thyme sprigs, leaves picked
3 or 4 white-fleshed peaches
275ml double cream
1 tbsp icing sugar, or to taste
finely grated zest of ½ lemon

TO FINISH:
Candied orange zest (see page 183)
3 blanched almonds, grated (ideally on a microplane)
tiny mint leaves
Vanilla syrup (see page 180)

1 In a small bowl, whisk together the honey,
lemon thyme leaves and 2 tbsp warm water.

2 Halve and stone the peaches. Cut one into
wafer-thin slices, using a mandolin if possible.
Cut the rest of the peaches into 1cm dice. Lay
the peach slices in one side of a dish and spoon
the diced peach into the other side. Pour the
honey mixture over them, cover and chill for
30 minutes.

3 In a bowl, lightly whip the cream with the
icing sugar until it holds soft peaks, then fold
in the grated lemon zest.

THIS IS A SIMPLE, NO-FUSS, YET GORGEOUS
DESSERT. MARINATING THE PEACHES WITH
HONEY AND LEMON THYME ADDS A SCENTED,
SOPHISTICATED TOUCH.

Peach Melba

SERVES **4**

170g raspberries
200ml white wine
1 tbsp sugar
2 tbsp thin honey
1 tsp vanilla extract
4 peaches, peeled and stoned
4 scoops of Vanilla ice cream (see page 181)

TO FINISH:
1 tbsp flaked almonds, lightly toasted if preferred
mint leaves
Vanilla syrup (see page 180)

1 Halve the raspberries, place them in a bowl and set aside.

2 Pour the white wine into a saucepan and add 200ml water, the sugar, honey and vanilla extract. Bring to the boil, stirring occasionally. Add the peaches and bring back to a simmer. Lower the heat and poach gently for about 5 minutes until the peaches are just tender. Lift them out with a slotted spoon onto a plate and peel away the skins, using a small knife. Cover and chill. Keep the poaching liquor.

3 Spoon about 3–4 tbsp of the poaching liquor over the raspberries, mix gently and set aside.

I'VE DECONSTRUCTED THIS CLASSIC DESSERT, AS I DO WITH A LOT OF MY DISHES AT THE RESTAURANT. RASPBERRIES, VANILLA AND PEACHES ARE A MARRIAGE MADE IN HEAVEN.

Place 2 peach halves on each plate
and scoop a ball of ice cream into one
half. Arrange the raspberries over and
around the peaches and scatter some
flaked almonds and mint leaves on top.
Finish with a drizzle of vanilla syrup.

Divide the strawberries between
serving bowls and add a few scoops
of strawberry sorbet. Serve at once,
pouring the melon soup into the
bowls at the table, and finishing with
a drizzle of vanilla syrup if you like.

Thyme-scented strawberries with melon soup and strawberry sorbet

SERVES **4**

200g strawberries, hulled
1 tbsp icing sugar
3 lemon thyme sprigs, leaves picked

MELON SOUP:
1 Cantaloupe melon
1–2 tbsp icing sugar, to taste

TO SERVE:
8–12 small scoops of Strawberry sorbet (see page 182)
Vanilla syrup (see page 180), to drizzle (optional)

1 Cut the strawberries into quarters or eighths, depending on size, and place in a bowl. Add the icing sugar and thyme leaves and mix gently. Cover and chill.

2 Halve the melon, scoop out the seeds and cut the flesh away from the skin. Purée the melon flesh in a blender until smooth. Add the icing sugar (adjust according to the sweetness of the melon). Pass through a fine sieve into a bowl, pressing down on the pulp to extract all of the juice. Pour into a serving jug, cover and chill.

THE SUCCESS OF THIS DISH RELIES ON THE FRESHNESS AND RIPENESS OF THE FRUITS. FOR ME, THIS IS ONE OF THE BEST DESSERTS IN THE BOOK – SIMPLE PERHAPS, BUT THE FLAVOUR PROFILE IS IMMENSE.

Plum and apple bruschetta with crème fraîche

PLUM AND APPLE COMPOTE:
2 Granny Smith apples
5 red plums
100g granulated or caster sugar

BRIOCHE BASE:
3 large eggs
20g caster sugar
300ml milk
few knobs of butter
8 thick slices of brioche

TO FINISH:
icing sugar, to dust
4 tbsp crème fraîche
4 tbsp maple syrup

1 For the compote, peel, halve and core the apples and cut into 2cm cubes. Halve and stone the plums and cut into similar-sized pieces.

2 Put the apples, sugar and 75ml water into a large heavy-based pan and bring to a simmer over a medium heat. Cook, stirring often with a wooden spoon, for about 4 minutes, then add the plums. Cook, stirring frequently, for about 5 minutes until softened. Lower the heat and let simmer to thicken slightly, stirring occasionally. Remove from the heat.

3 For the brioche base, in a large bowl, whisk together the eggs, sugar and milk. One at a time, dip in the brioche slices, coating both sides and allowing the mixture to be absorbed slightly. Gently shake off any excess liquid and place on a wire rack to drain.

4 Heat a large non-stick frying pan with a few knobs of butter over a medium-low heat. Fry the brioche slices until golden brown, about 2–3 minutes on each side.

A FUN DESSERT THAT WORKS EQUALLY
WELL AS A LAZY WEEKEND BRUNCH DISH.
THE FRUIT COMPOTE FREEZES WELL –
IT'S A HANDY TOPPING FOR ICE CREAM,
YOGHURT OR PANCAKES.

Dust the brioche slices with icing sugar. Place 2 slices on each plate, one on top of the other at an angle. Spoon on some of the plum and apple compote and top with a neat spoonful of crème fraîche. Drizzle maple syrup decoratively around the plate.

Arrange 4 apricot halves on each plate. Spoon the yoghurt decoratively on top and around the apricots. Sprinkle with some of the pistachios and top with the lemon zest and mint. Add a drizzle of honey. Serve the extra yoghurt in a bowl on the side, topped with the rest of the pistachios and a drizzle of honey.

Yoghurt with apricots, honey and pistachios

SERVES **4**

400g Greek yoghurt
3 tbsp icing sugar, sifted
1 lemon
320ml dry white wine
3 tbsp thin honey
120g caster sugar
8 apricots, halved and stoned
2 tsp orange flower water
2 tbsp pistachio nuts, chopped

TO FINISH:
tiny mint leaves
2 tbsp thin honey

1 Mix the yoghurt and icing sugar together in a bowl, cover and chill.

2 Using a swivel vegetable peeler, finely pare the zest from the lemon in wide ribbons, then squeeze the juice.

3 Put the white wine, lemon zest and juice, honey and sugar into a saucepan and slowly bring to the boil, stirring until the sugar is dissolved. Reduce the heat to a simmer and add the apricots. Poach until just softened, about 5 minutes. Remove the apricots with a slotted spoon and place in a bowl.

4 Continue to simmer the wine syrup until reduced down by a third. Take out the lemon zest and reserve. Set the syrup aside to cool. Once cooled, mix in the orange flower water and pour over the apricots. Cover and chill for at least 2 hours.

5 Meanwhile, lightly toast the chopped pistachios in a dry frying pan over a low heat for a few minutes until fragrant. Tip into a bowl and set aside.

THIS FRAGRANT DESSERT EPITOMISES GREEK FOOD
AT ITS BEST – SIMPLE INGREDIENTS THAT WORK
TOGETHER BEAUTIFULLY AND LOOK STUNNING.

Poached autumn fruits in warm sangria

SERVES **4**

SANGRIA:

750ml red wine

200g frozen mixed berries

1¼ tsp (3g) ground coffee

100g caster sugar, or to taste

POACHED AUTUMN FRUIT:

2 red plums

1 green apple

1 pear

4 ripe, but firm figs

1 vanilla pod, cut in half and split lengthways

finely pared zest of ½ lemon

finely pared zest of ½ orange

1 For the sangria, put the wine, frozen berries, ground coffee and sugar into a large saucepan. Bring to the boil, stirring to encourage the sugar to dissolve, then lower the heat and simmer very gently for 10 minutes. Take off the heat and set aside to infuse for 45 minutes.

2 Pass the sangria mixture through a fine sieve into a bowl, pressing the pulp with the back of a ladle to extract all the juice. Pour the liquor back into the pan.

3 To prepare the fruit, halve and stone the plums, quarter and core the apple and pear, and cut the figs in half.

4 Scrape the seeds from the vanilla pod and add them to the sangria with the empty pod pieces and citrus zest strips. Bring to a low simmer and then add the fruit. Cook gently for about 8 minutes until just tender. Take off the heat and let cool slightly. Taste for sweetness, adding a bit more sugar if needed. Serve warm.

SANGRIA ACQUIRED A POOR REPUTATION HERE IN THE 70S AND 80S, WHEN IT WAS REGARDED AS A CHEAP THING TO DRINK ON DODGY HOLIDAYS IN BENIDORM. WHEN MADE PROPERLY, HOWEVER, IT TASTES FANTASTIC.

Ladle the fruit and sangria into individual bowls
and top with a vanilla pod piece, if you like.

Spiced pineapple with coconut sorbet and candied ginger

SERVES **4**

SPICED PINEAPPLE:

½ pineapple (cut lengthways)

250g granulated or caster sugar

1 vanilla pod

10g fresh root ginger, peeled and chopped

1 lemongrass stalk, trimmed and cut into
    2cm pieces

2g cloves

5g black peppercorns

2 star anise pods

CANDIED GINGER:

12g fresh root ginger, peeled

200g caster sugar, plus more for coating

TO SERVE:

4 scoops of Coconut sorbet (see page 181)

small handful of tiny coriander leaves

1 Trim and peel the pineapple half. Cut it lengthways in half again and remove the core. Now slice the pineapple in half crossways. Using a sharp knife, slice the halves thinly lengthways into 5mm thick slices. You need 20–24 slices.

2 Melt the sugar in a large heavy-based pan over a medium heat, stirring gently to ensure it melts evenly. Increase the heat slightly and cook until the melted sugar forms a dark caramel. Reduce the heat to medium low and add the vanilla pod, ginger, lemongrass and spices. Stir over the heat for about 1 minute. Now stir in 75ml water, taking care as the hot caramel will splutter.

3 Lay the pineapple slices in the spiced caramel and cook, flipping the slices over often, for 3–4 minutes until softened, but retaining their shape. Remove from the heat.

4 Carefully transfer the pineapple slices to a large dish, making sure they are completely submerged in the caramel. Leave to stand for 24 hours at room temperature.

5 To prepare the ginger, finely slice the root ginger on a mandolin if possible. Bring a small pan of water to the boil and blanch the ginger slices for 1–2 minutes, then drain. Repeat this process 3 times, changing the water each time, to mellow the sharp spiciness.

6 To candy the ginger slices, place the sugar in a saucepan with 200ml water and slowly bring to the boil, stirring to dissolve the sugar. Add the blanched ginger and allow to simmer over a medium-low heat for 4–5 minutes. Remove with a slotted spoon and drain on a wire rack. Cool slightly, then toss in a little caster sugar to coat. Leave to dry at room temperature for about an hour until crisp.

PINEAPPLE MARRIES WELL WITH SO MANY FLAVOURS. HERE I'VE COOKED THIN SLICES
IN A CARAMEL FLAVOURED WITH SPICES, BUT YOU MIGHT LIKE TO TRY ROASTING IT WITH
RED CHILLIES FOR A MORE UNUSUAL TWIST.

TO PLATE

Using a slotted spoon, arrange 5 or 6 pineapple slices on each plate and drizzle with the spiced caramel sauce. Top with a scoop of coconut sorbet and decorate with candied ginger and coriander leaves.

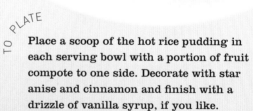

TO PLATE

Place a scoop of the hot rice pudding in each serving bowl with a portion of fruit compote to one side. Decorate with star anise and cinnamon and finish with a drizzle of vanilla syrup, if you like.

Rice pudding with winter fruit compote

SERVES **4–6**

RICE PUDDING:
100g unsalted butter
180g pudding rice
120g golden caster sugar
850ml whole milk
150ml double cream

WINTER FRUIT COMPOTE:
2 Braeburn or other crisp apples
2 pears
10 prunes
20g dark brown sugar
1 cinnamon stick
2 star anise pods
50ml dark rum

TO FINISH (OPTIONAL):
handful of star anise pods
few cinnamon sticks, halved
Vanilla syrup (see page 180), optional

1 For the rice pudding, preheat the oven to 140°C/Gas 1. Melt the butter in a large heavy-based ovenproof cooking pot over a low heat. Add the rice, sugar, milk and cream. Slowly bring to the boil, then take off the heat and stir to distribute the rice evenly over the bottom of the pan. Bake in the oven for 75–90 minutes until the pudding has just set and a skin has formed on the surface; do not stir.

2 Meanwhile, make the fruit compote. Quarter, core and dice the apples and pears. Place in a medium saucepan with the prunes, sugar, cinnamon, star anise and rum. Cook gently, stirring occasionally, for about 8–10 minutes until the fruit is just softened and the juices have reduced and thickened.

I HAVE BASED THIS ON MY MUM'S RICE PUDDING, WHICH HAD A WONDERFUL WARMING QUALITY. IT WAS ONE OF THE FEW DISHES I LOVED EATING AS A CHILD. AT AN EARLY AGE, FOOD WAS A CHORE RATHER THAN A PASSION FOR ME... HOW THINGS HAVE CHANGED.

Banana cake with lemongrass and ginger custard

MAKES ABOUT **10** SLICES

135g unsalted butter, plus extra to grease
   the tin
2 ripe medium bananas (to yield about
   210g once mashed)
finely grated zest of 1 lemon
160g self-raising flour
1 tsp baking powder
pinch of salt
105g caster sugar
1 large egg, beaten
4 tbsp golden syrup

LEMONGRASS AND GINGER CUSTARD:

475ml double cream
10g fresh root ginger, cut into 1cm pieces
1 lemongrass stalk, cut into 3cm pieces
6 large egg yolks
70g caster sugar

TO SERVE:

1 banana
icing sugar, to dust
2 lemon thyme sprigs, leaves picked

1 Preheat the oven to 180°C/Gas 4. Grease a 23x13cm (900g) loaf tin and line it with buttered greaseproof paper, leaving a 4cm overhang on both sides to act as handles.

2 Mash the bananas in a bowl, using a fork, and mix in the lemon zest. Sift the flour, baking powder and salt together into a bowl and set aside.

3 Beat the butter and sugar together, using an electric mixer, until light and fluffy. Beat in the egg and golden syrup, then add the mashed bananas and mix well. Finally add the sifted flour mixture and fold together using a rubber spatula until evenly combined.

4 Spoon the mixture evenly into the loaf tin and bake for 45–55 minutes until a skewer inserted in the middle comes out clean. Leave to cool in the tin for 15 minutes.

5 To make the custard, pour the cream into a heavy-based saucepan and add the ginger and lemongrass. Bring to a simmer, then take off the heat and leave to infuse for 10 minutes. Meanwhile, whisk the egg yolks and sugar together in a bowl. Remove the ginger and lemongrass from the cream with a slotted spoon, then bring back almost to a simmer. Slowly trickle the hot cream onto the egg mix, whisking constantly. Return to a low heat and cook, stirring with a wooden spoon, until the custard thickens enough to coat the back of the spoon. Pour into a serving jug; keep warm.

6 Lift the banana cake out of the tin onto a wire rack, removing the paper. Allow to cool.

7 When ready to assemble, slice the banana on the diagonal into 2cm thick pieces and dust generously with icing sugar. Caramelise using a cook's blowtorch or quickly under a hot grill.

CARAMELISED BANANAS AND A FRAGRANT LEMONGRASS
AND GINGER CUSTARD GIVE AN EVERYDAY CAKE AN
EXOTIC TWIST. SAVE ANY EXTRA CUSTARD TO POUR OVER
ICE CREAM FOR AN EASY DESSERT THE FOLLOWING DAY.

Cut 1 or 2 slices of banana cake per serving and place on each plate. Pour on some custard and arrange a few caramelised banana slices on the cake and around the plate. Finish with a sprinkling of lemon thyme and a final dusting of icing sugar. Serve the extra custard in a jug.

Carefully cut each pudding in half
to reveal the filling. Place a scoop of
clotted cream in the middle and top
with the reserved vanilla pod pieces.
Finish with a drizzle of vanilla syrup,
if you like.

Autumn pudding with clotted cream

SERVES **4**

1 Gala apple
1 Granny Smith apple
1 pear
3 plums
juice of ½ lemon
1–2 vanilla pods, cut in half and split lengthways
3 tbsp thin, dark honey
8–10 slices of brioche, crusts removed

TO FINISH:
4 tbsp clotted cream
Vanilla syrup (see page 180), to drizzle (optional)

1 Quarter, core and dice the apples and pear; halve, stone and dice the plums. Place the fruit in a large saucepan with the lemon juice. Scrape the seeds from the vanilla pod(s) and add to the pan together with the empty pod pieces. Bring to a simmer over a medium heat, stirring occasionally, then lower the heat and simmer for about 10 minutes until softened. Stir in the honey and leave to cool slightly. Remove and reserve the vanilla pod pieces.

2 Line four small individual pudding basins (or dariole moulds) with cling film. Now line the basins with the brioche slices, cutting them to fit as necessary and making sure there are no gaps.

3 Spoon the fruit into the bread-lined basins, pressing down firmly to avoid air pockets and filling to the brim. Cover the top of each pudding with a layer of bread slices and place a disc of greaseproof paper on top. Set a small plate on top of each pudding and weight it down. Chill overnight.

4 To unmould, uncover the puddings and invert an individual serving plate on top of each one. Carefully, but quickly, turn the puddings over, using the cling film to help pop them out onto the plate.

SUMMER PUDDING – SOFT FRUITS ENCASED IN BREAD STAINED RED OR PURPLE WITH THE BERRY JUICES – IS A CLASSIC BRITISH DESSERT, BUT AUTUMN FRUITS CAN BE USED IN THE SAME WAY. I USE BRIOCHE RATHER THAN PLAIN BREAD AND SERVE THE PUDDING WITH CLOTTED CREAM FOR A TOUCH OF LUXURY.

Baked apples and sultanas

75g sultanas
120ml dark rum
25g butter
15g caster sugar
4 Pink Lady apples

CRUMBLE TOPPING:
125g plain flour
45g granulated sugar
65g butter, cubed
a little beaten egg (about ¼ egg)

TO SERVE:
Vanilla crème anglaise (see page 180)
Vanilla syrup (see page 180), to drizzle (optional)
small mint leaves, to finish

1 Put the sultanas and rum into a small pan and bring to the boil. Immediately remove from the heat and set aside to macerate for 30 minutes. Preheat the oven to 180°C/Gas 4.

2 Meanwhile, make the crumble topping. Sift the flour into a bowl and stir in the sugar. Add the butter cubes and rub together with your fingertips until the mixture resembles coarse crumbs. Drizzle in the egg slowly and mix until crumbly. Tip onto a tray and chill until firm, about 15 minutes.

3 Melt the 25g butter in a small saucepan over a low heat and stir in the caster sugar. Core the apples, using an apple corer, and then cut them in half across the middle.

4 Brush the apples with the warm sugary butter and place them, rounded side down, on a baking tray. Bake for 10–15 minutes until just softening.

5 Remove the sultanas from the rum with a slotted spoon and place in a blender. Purée to a compote consistency, adding a little of the rum if necessary. Spoon the blended sultanas into the apple half cavities.

6 Spoon a generous amount of the crumble on top of each apple (freeze the rest for another pudding). Return the apples to the oven and bake for a further 8–10 minutes until the crumble topping is golden brown.

I PLAY AROUND A LOT WITH CLASSIC PUDDINGS AND THIS
IS MY VERSION OF AN APPLE CRUMBLE. MAKE IT IN THE
AUTUMN WHEN HOME-GROWN APPLES ARE ABUNDANT.

Place 2 apple halves on a plate and pour over a little of the crème anglaise. Add a drizzle of vanilla syrup, if you like, and finish with mint leaves. Hand the rest of the crème anglaise around in a jug.

Crisscross the rhubarb batons on the cheesecake and scatter over some of the ginger pieces and the mint leaves. Drizzle rhubarb syrup around the plate and on the cheesecake. Do the same with the vanilla syrup. Serve at once, with the extra ginger on the side.

Vanilla cheesecake with rhubarb and ginger

SERVES **4**

1 vanilla pod, split lengthways
150g granulated sugar
100ml whipping cream
250g cream cheese
85g caster sugar
juice of ½ lime
1½ trimmed rhubarb stalks, about 150g
50g pickled sliced ginger (from a jar)
60g grenadine
85g shortbread biscuits
15g butter, melted

TO FINISH:
small mint leaves
Vanilla syrup (see page 180), to drizzle

1 Scrape the seeds from one half of the vanilla pod and mix them with half of the granulated sugar in a bowl, using your fingers. Set aside.

2 Pour the cream into a bowl. Scrape the seeds from the other half of the vanilla pod and add them to the cream. Whip lightly to soft peaks.

3 In another bowl, whisk together the cream cheese, caster sugar and lime juice until smooth. Spoon in the whipped vanilla cream and fold together, using a spatula. Chill to firm up for about 30 minutes.

4 Meanwhile, cut the rhubarb into 8cm lengths and then into batons, about 5mm thick. Place in a bowl with the pickled ginger.

5 Put the rest of the granulated sugar and 200ml water in a small pan and dissolve over a medium heat. Add the grenadine and bring to the boil. Pour over the rhubarb and ginger and let steep for 10–15 minutes until the rhubarb is just tender but still holding its shape. Remove the ginger and rhubarb with a slotted spoon and dry on kitchen paper. Simmer the liquor over a medium-low heat for 8–10 minutes to reduce by two-thirds. Set aside.

6 Meanwhile, crush the shortbread in a plastic bag with a rolling pin to fine crumbs. Tip into a bowl and mix with the melted butter.

7 Pat the rhubarb sticks dry with kitchen paper and roll them gently in the vanilla sugar to coat. Place on a plate and set aside.

8 Assemble the individual cheesecakes just before serving. Shape a quarter of the shortbread crust into a round on each plate and flatten gently with the bottom of a glass. Scoop the cheesecake mixture neatly on top.

I LOVE COOKING WITH RHUBARB, WHETHER IT IS FOR A CRUMBLE, PIE OR ICE CREAM – OR POACHING IT IN A FLAVOURED SUGAR SYRUP AS I HAVE HERE. THIS ELEGANT DESSERT IS DECEPTIVELY EASY TO MAKE, YET GUARANTEED TO IMPRESS.

Contemporary marshmallow with mulled cherries

SERVES **4**

icing sugar, to dust
a little sunflower oil, to oil the moulds
3 large (or 5 small) sheets of leaf gelatine
350g granulated or caster sugar
30g liquid glucose
2 large egg whites
1 tsp vanilla extract

MULLED CHERRIES:

140g cherries (about 12)
400ml red wine
pared zest of ½ lemon and ½ orange
1 star anise pod
2 cloves
1 sachet of mulling spices
2 tbsp icing sugar, or to taste

TO FINISH:

baby basil leaves
Candied orange zest (see page 183)

1 Line a tray with baking parchment and dredge with icing sugar. Oil 4 ring moulds, 3.5cm in diameter and 4.5cm tall, and place on the tray. (If you don't have ring moulds, cut 4.5cm tall cylinders from a finished kitchen roll. Slit each one down the side, open out and wrap tightly in foil. Bring the ends together and crimp closed to form rings.)

2 Soak the leaf gelatine in cold water to cover until softened.

3 Put the sugar, liquid glucose and 50ml water into a small saucepan. Bring slowly to the boil, then increase the heat and boil until the syrup registers 127°C on a cooking thermometer, about 2–3 minutes. In the meantime, whisk the egg whites with an electric mixer on high speed until they form firm peaks.

4 Drain the gelatine, squeeze out excess water and whisk into the egg whites. Immediately reduce the whisk speed to medium and pour in the hot sugar syrup down the side of the bowl. Now whisk at high speed until the base of the bowl has cooled to room temperature, about 5 minutes. The marshmallow should be fluffy and stiff enough to hold peaks easily.

5 Scoop the marshmallow into a large plastic bag and seal. Cut off one corner and pipe into the ring moulds. With a finger dipped in icing sugar, tap down any peaks to give a flat top. (Any leftover marshmallow can be piped onto the tray and cut into pieces for sweets.) Leave to set at room temperature, about 20 minutes.

6 To prepare the cherries, stone and quarter them. Pour the red wine into a saucepan, add the citrus zests, spices and mulling spice sachet and bring to the boil. Take off the heat and cool slightly, then strain into a bowl. Add the cherries and sweeten with icing sugar to taste. Allow to cool to room temperature, then cover and chill.

7 Unmould each marshmallow by warming the ring mould in your hands (or uncrimping the foil), then spear on a stick and toast over a gas flame to caramelise slightly.

WE HAVE SOME OF THE SWEETEST CHERRIES IN THE WORLD IN THE UK AND I LIKE TO MAKE THE MOST OF THEM WHEN THEY ARE IN SEASON AT THE HEIGHT OF THE SUMMER. THIS IS A FUN WAY TO SERVE THEM.

Place a toasted marshmallow in the centre of each wide serving bowl. Spoon the cherries around the marshmallow and finish with baby basil leaves and candied orange zest.

Carefully split the meringues. Spoon some lemon and lime curd into the bottom shell, drizzle with passion fruit syrup and spoon more syrup around the meringue. Replace the top. Serve the rest of the curd in a bowl on the side, sprinkled with pink peppercorns and candied zest.

Pink peppercorn meringues with lemon and lime curd

SERVES **4**

PINK PEPPERCORN SYRUP:
1 tsp pink peppercorns, cracked
1 tbsp Vanilla syrup (see page 180)

MERINGUES:
100g egg whites (2–3 eggs, depending on size)
100g caster sugar
100g icing sugar, sifted

PASSION FRUIT SYRUP:
2 passion fruit
20g granulated or caster sugar

LEMON AND LIME CURD:
juice of 2 lemons (save the zest)
juice of 2 limes (save the zest)
80g caster sugar
80g eggs (about 2 large), beaten
80g egg yolks (4 medium)
80g butter, diced

TO FINISH:
½ tsp pink peppercorns
Candied lime and lemon zest (see page 183,
  use the zest from the above fruit)

1 Preheat the oven to 90°C/Gas ¼ and line a baking sheet with baking parchment.

2 For the peppercorn syrup, mix the cracked pink peppercorns with the vanilla syrup in a small bowl; set aside.

3 To make the meringues, using an electric mixer, whisk the egg whites with 2 tbsp caster sugar on high speed until thickened. Whisk in the remaining caster sugar, 1 tbsp at a time. Keep whisking until the meringue is stiff, shiny and holding firm peaks, about 4–6 minutes. Now, with a large spatula, carefully fold in the icing sugar a quarter at a time.

4 Spoon the meringue into 4 mounds on the lined baking sheet, making a curling peak on top of each one. Dry in the oven for 40 minutes or until the outer shell has just hardened.

5 Take out the meringues and brush gently with peppercorn syrup. Return to the oven for another 1–1½ hours until they are dry and easily peel off the paper.

6 For the passion fruit syrup, scoop out the flesh and seeds from the fruit into a small pan and mix in the sugar. Simmer over a medium-low heat to dissolve the sugar, about 2–3 minutes. Pour into a small bowl and chill.

7 To make the lemon and lime curd, put the citrus juices in a heavy-based pan with the sugar. Dissolve over a medium heat, bring to the boil, then take off the heat. In a bowl, whisk the whole eggs and yolks together, then pour in the hot citrus syrup in a thin steady stream, whisking constantly. Return to the pan and place over a low heat. Whisk in the butter a piece at a time, then stir over the heat for 4–6 minutes until the curd thickens. Pour into a bowl, cover the surface with cling film to prevent a skin from forming and chill.

THIS COMBINATION OF FLAVOURS IS A LITTLE UNUSUAL, BUT THE
HEAT OF THE PEPPERS REALLY WORKS WITH SWEET MERINGUES.
SAVE ANY LEFTOVER CITRUS CURD TO SPREAD ON CRUMPETS.

Peanut butter and strawberry jam parfait

MAKES **8**

BRICELET:
25g unsalted butter
10ml double cream
30g caster sugar
10g liquid glucose
30g flaked almonds, roughly chopped
vegetable oil, to oil the moulds

PEANUT BUTTER PARFAIT:
45g smooth peanut butter
10ml frangelico (hazelnut liqueur) or amaretto
  di Saronno
105ml double cream
2 large eggs, 1 separated
45g caster sugar

TO SERVE:
2 tsp strawberry jam
8 tiny scoops of Strawberry sorbet (see page 182)

1 For the bricelet, put the butter, cream, sugar and liquid glucose into a large saucepan over a medium heat and stir until melted. Take off the heat and stir in the almonds. Turn onto a baking sheet lined with baking parchment, cover with another sheet of parchment and roll out to a thin layer. Chill for 20 minutes or so.

2 Preheat the oven to 160°C/Gas 3. Lightly oil eight 4cm diameter ring moulds (or make your own, see page 148) and set on a tray.

3 Remove the top sheet of paper and bake the bricelet for about 8 minutes until golden brown. Let cool slightly until just warm, then cut out 16 rounds, using a 4cm pastry cutter. If it becomes too firm to cut, warm in the oven. Place a round in the bottom of each ring mould.

4 For the parfait, in a small bowl, mix the peanut butter, liqueur and 30ml of the cream together to a smooth paste. Cover and chill. Lightly whip the remaining 75ml cream until softly peaking, cover and chill.

5 Using an electric mixer, whisk the whole egg and second egg yolk together on high speed. Heat 30g of the sugar and 1 tbsp water in a small saucepan until dissolved and syrupy, about 2 minutes. Slowly trickle the syrup onto the eggs, whisking constantly. Continue to whisk until the mixture is fluffy and almost white, and the bottom of the bowl no longer feels warm. Set aside.

6 In another large bowl, whisk the egg white until peaking, then whisk in the remaining 15g sugar, a little at a time until soft peaks form. Fold in the semi-whipped cream, followed by the whisked egg and sugar mix. Finally fold in the peanut butter mixture.

7 Spoon or pipe the parfait into the ring moulds, taking care to avoid air pockets. Gently level the tops with a knife. Place in the freezer to set for at least an hour. Allow to soften at room temperature for 5 minutes or so before serving.

I INVENTED THIS PARFAIT AS A STYLISH SLANT ON A PEANUT BUTTER AND JAM SANDWICH FIVE YEARS AGO AND IT SOON BECAME A FIRM FAVOURITE AT THE RESTAURANT. THIS IS A SIMPLIFIED VERSION FOR THE HOME COOK.

Unmould the parfaits by gently warming the ring moulds in your hands or very briefly with a cook's blowtorch. Carefully spoon about ¼ tsp jam on top of each parfait and cover with another round of bricelet. Lift each parfait onto a serving plate and top with a neat oval of strawberry sorbet.

Vanilla panna cotta with tomato and passion fruit syrup

SERVES **4**

PANNA COTTA:
2 large (or 3½ small) sheets of leaf gelatine
260ml double cream
110ml milk
½ vanilla pod, split lengthways
45g caster sugar

TOMATO AND PASSION FRUIT SYRUP:
100g caster sugar
3 plum tomatoes
4 passion fruit, halved
splash of cherry brandy

TO FINISH:
tiny mint sprigs

1 Soak the leaf gelatine in cold water to cover until softened. Set aside.

2 Pour the cream and milk into a heavy-based saucepan. Scrape the seeds from the vanilla pod and add them to the pan with the empty pod and the sugar. Slowly bring to the boil, then remove from the heat and discard the vanilla pod. Squeeze the softened gelatine to remove the excess water, then add to the hot cream mixture and stir until dissolved.

3 Carefully pour the creamy mixture into 4 ramekins and allow to cool, then refrigerate for 3 hours or until set.

4 Meanwhile, make the tomato and passion fruit syrup. Preheat the oven to 110°C/Gas ¼. Put 100ml water and the sugar into a small pan and slowly bring to the boil, stirring to dissolve the sugar and make a simple sugar syrup; set aside.

5 Bring a pan of salted water to the boil and have a bowl of iced water ready. Score a shallow cross on the bottom of each tomato. Blanch the tomatoes in the boiling water for 2 minutes, then immediately remove and immerse in the iced water. Peel the skins off carefully in quarters and reserve. Dice the tomatoes and place in a bowl.

6 Line a baking tray with a silicone liner (Silpat). Dip the tomato skins in the sugar syrup and lay them on the liner. Place in the oven for 20–30 minutes to dry.

7 Meanwhile, scoop the pulp and seeds from the passion fruit and add them to the pan containing the sugar syrup, along with the diced tomatoes. Bring to a simmer and cook over a medium-low heat for 15–20 minutes, stirring occasionally, until reduced and thickened. Finally, add the cherry brandy.

8 When ready to serve, unmould each panna cotta: run a thin knife around the inside of the ramekin, then briefly dip in a bowl of hot water for 3–4 seconds and flip over onto a serving plate. Shake carefully to loosen and turn out.

AS TOMATOES ARE FRUIT, IT SEEMS NATURAL TO ME TO USE THEM IN A DESSERT. PAIRING A CREAMY PANNA COTTA WITH A SYRUP MADE FROM PLUM TOMATOES AND TART PASSION FRUIT WORKS BRILLIANTLY.

TO PLATE

Arrange the tomato skins decoratively
on top of the panna cottas and drizzle the
tomato and passion fruit syrup around.
Finish with a few tiny mint sprigs.

Coconut bread pudding

SERVES **4**

4 large eggs, beaten
135g caster sugar
270ml double cream
270ml coconut milk
2 tsp dark rum
7 slices of brioche

TO FINISH:
a wedge of fresh coconut (about 15g)
icing sugar, to dust

1 In a large bowl, whisk the eggs and sugar together until smooth and pale. Pour the cream into a heavy-based saucepan and slowly bring almost to a simmer, then take off the heat and gradually whisk into the egg mixture. Return to a low heat and whisk in the coconut milk and rum. Cook gently, stirring with a wooden spoon, until the mixture is thick enough to coat the back of the spoon lightly; do not allow to boil. Remove from the heat and set aside.

2 Preheat the oven to 140°C/Gas 1. Cut the brioche slices in half on the diagonal. Arrange the brioche triangles, points upwards, in a baking dish (or in 2 small oval baking dishes) to form overlapping rows. Pour the custard evenly over the surface.

3 Stand the dish(es) in a roasting tin and pour in enough hot water to come halfway up the sides of the dish(es). Bake for about 35 minutes until just set.

4 In the meantime, shave the coconut into fine ribbons, using a vegetable peeler.

5 When the pudding is ready, lift it out of the water bath. Dust the surface generously with icing sugar and caramelise using a cook's blowtorch or by flashing under a hot grill for a minute or so.

TO PLATE

Dust the surface of the pudding with a little more icing sugar and scatter over the fresh coconut shavings. Serve from the dish.

THE SIMPLE ADDITION OF COCONUT AND A DASH OF RUM TAKES A SIMPLE BREAD AND BUTTER PUDDING TO A NEW LEVEL.

Brazo de mercedes with passion fruit sauce

MAKES ABOUT **6** SLICES

PASSION FRUIT SAUCE:
2 passion fruit
1 tbsp icing sugar

FILLING:
500ml milk
100g caster or granulated sugar
1 tbsp unsalted butter
2 tsp vanilla extract
4 large egg yolks, beaten
50g cashew nuts, toasted and finely ground
2 tsp cornflour

MERINGUE:
a little unsalted butter, to grease the tray
5 large egg whites
¼ tsp cream of tartar
50g caster sugar
1 tsp vanilla extract

TO FINISH:
1 tbsp icing sugar, to dust
tiny mint leaves

1 For the passion fruit sauce, halve the passion fruit and scoop out the pulp and seeds into a bowl. Add the icing sugar and stir until dissolved. Cover and chill.

2 To make the filling, pour the milk into a heavy-based saucepan, bring to the boil and simmer over a medium-low heat until reduced by half, about 10 minutes. Stir in the sugar, butter and vanilla extract. Remove from the heat and let cool slightly for a minute, then slowly add the egg yolks in a thin stream, whisking constantly. Whisk in the ground cashew nuts and cornflour.

3 Return the pan to a low heat and cook, stirring, until the mixture is a paste-like consistency, about 3–4 minutes. Pour onto a tray, cover with cling film and chill.

4 For the meringue, preheat the oven to 200°C/ Gas 6. Butter a small 2cm deep baking tray, about 20 x 15cm (or half a standard 41x 30cm tray). Line with greaseproof paper and butter the paper well.

5 Using an electric mixer, whisk the egg whites and cream of tartar on high speed until stiff, then gradually whisk in the sugar. Continue to whisk until the meringue is glossy and holds stiff peaks, then fold in the vanilla extract using a spatula.

6 Spread the meringue evenly on the greased paper with a palette knife. Bake for 10 minutes until the top is evenly golden brown and the meringue is puffed up. Set aside to cool.

7 Once cooled, invert the meringue onto a large board and peel off the greaseproof paper. Spread the filling evenly over the entire meringue and then carefully roll the meringue up from one end to form a log. Chill until ready to serve.

SOUTHEAST ASIA IS NOT KNOWN FOR DESSERTS, BUT THIS RECIPE, WHICH I DISCOVERED IN THE PHILIPPINES, IS ENTICING. IT CUTS INTO 6 SLICES – ENOUGH FOR SECONDS.

Cut the log into 6 slices and arrange cut
side up on a serving platter. Drizzle with the
passion fruit sauce and dust with icing sugar.
Finish with mint leaves and serve at once.

Just before serving, dust the tart with icing sugar and cut into slices. Place a slice on each serving plate and top with a neat spoonful of fromage frais. Drizzle decoratively with vanilla syrup, if you like, and finish with mint leaves.

Treacle tart

MAKES **6–8** SLICES

PASTRY:

225g plain flour, plus extra to dust

pinch of salt

100g butter, cubed, plus extra to grease the tin

20g caster sugar

1 large egg yolk

FILLING:

140ml double cream

1 medium egg

310g golden syrup

85g fresh white breadcrumbs

55g ground almonds

TO SERVE:

icing sugar, to dust

4 tbsp fromage frais or Vanilla ice cream (see page 181)

Vanilla syrup (see page 180), to drizzle (optional)

small mint leaves, to finish

---

1 To make the pastry, sift the flour and salt into a large bowl, add the butter and rub together with your fingertips until the mixture resembles crumbs. Stir in the sugar. Beat the egg yolk with 25ml water, then gradually mix into the crumb mixture until the dough begins to hold together. Gather the dough and press into a flat disc. Wrap in cling film and chill for at least 1 hour.

2 Lightly grease a loose-bottomed 20cm tart tin with butter. Roll out the dough thinly on a floured surface to a circle, 5mm thick. Line the tart tin with the pastry, pressing it well into the edges and cutting away the excess overhanging the rim. Chill while you prepare the filling.

3 Preheat the oven to 180°C/Gas 4. To make the filling, whisk the cream and egg together in a large bowl. Warm the golden syrup in a saucepan over a low heat, stirring constantly, then pour onto the cream mixture, whisking all the time. Stir in the breadcrumbs and ground almonds.

4 Pour the filling into the pastry case and spread it evenly. Bake the tart in the oven for 35–40 minutes until the filling is just set and the pastry is golden brown.

I HAVE FOND MEMORIES OF TREACLE TART. WHEN I WAS A CHILD IT WAS ALWAYS A TOSS UP BETWEEN A BAKEWELL AND A TREACLE TART FROM OUR LOCAL BAKERY. ALTHOUGH IT'S VERY RICH, I STILL LIKE THE COMPLETE AND UTTER SUGAR HIT THIS TART DELIVERS. IT IS WELL WORTH THE TOTAL INDULGENCE.

Crème brûlée with prunes in Armagnac

SERVES **4–6**

MACERATED PRUNES:
50ml Armagnac
15g caster sugar
½ vanilla pod, split lengthways
2 star anise pods
4 juniper berries
150g prunes (12–18)

CRÈME BRÛLÉES:
300ml double cream
120ml milk
½ vanilla pod, split lengthways
4 large egg yolks
50g caster sugar

TO FINISH:
4–6 tbsp golden caster sugar

1 Prepare the prunes a day ahead. Put the Armagnac, sugar and 80ml water into a saucepan. Scrape the seeds from the vanilla pod and add them to the pan together with the empty half-pod, star anise and juniper berries. Slowly bring to the boil. Tip the prunes into a bowl and pour the hot liquor and aromatics over them. Leave to steep at room temperature for 24 hours.

2 For the crème brûlées, preheat the oven to 120°C/Gas ½. Pour the cream and milk into a heavy-based saucepan. Scrape the seeds from the vanilla pod and add them to the pan with the empty half-pod. Bring almost to a simmer over a low heat. Meanwhile, whisk the egg yolks and sugar together in a bowl until pale. Slowly pour the hot cream mixture onto the egg and sugar mix, whisking constantly.

3 Place the pan back over a very low heat and cook, stirring constantly with a wooden spoon, until slightly thickened, about 3–4 minutes. Discard the vanilla pod. Pour the custard into 4–6 ramekins.

4 Stand the ramekins in a roasting tin. Pour in enough hot water to come about two-thirds of the way up the sides of the dishes. Bake in the oven for 20–25 minutes (depending on the size of the ramekins) until just set, but still wobbly in the middle. Remove the ramekins from the water bath and allow to cool, then chill in the fridge for 3 hours until set.

5 Sprinkle a thin, even layer of caster sugar over the top of each brûlée and caramelise using a cook's blowtorch or by placing under a hot grill for 30 seconds or so.

EVERYONE HAS THEIR OWN FAVOURITE VERSION OF CRÈME BRÛLÉE AND THIS IS MINE. STEEPING PRUNES IN ARMAGNAC WITH STAR ANISE, JUNIPER AND VANILLA GIVES THEM A FANTASTIC FLAVOUR. HERE THEY CONTRAST AND COMPLEMENT THE CREAMY BRÛLÉE PERFECTLY.

TO PLATE

Using a slotted spoon, place
3 or 4 prunes on top of each
brûlée and serve at once.

Paris Brest with cobnuts

SERVES **4**

CHOUX PASTRY:
60g unsalted butter, plus extra for the paper
85g strong white bread flour
½ tsp caster sugar
pinch of salt
3 large eggs, beaten

GLAZE:
1 egg, beaten (or any leftover from the pastry)
pinch of salt

CHOCOLATE AND HAZELNUT FILLING:
250ml double cream
55g chocolate hazelnut spread, such as Nutella

TO FINISH:
25g cobnuts, shelled, sliced and lightly toasted
icing sugar, to dust
Vanilla syrup (see page 180), to drizzle (optional)

1 Preheat the oven to 200°C/Gas 6. Line a baking sheet with baking parchment, draw a 6cm circle on the paper and flip it over. Secure the underside corners with a smear of butter.

2 To make the choux pastry, sift the flour, sugar and salt together into a bowl; set aside. Put the butter and 100ml water into a heavy-based saucepan and bring to the boil over a medium heat. Take off the heat, quickly tip the flour mixture into the pan, and beat with a wooden spoon until smooth. Return to the heat to cook and dry out, stirring, until the dough comes away from the sides of the pan and forms a ball, about 3–4 minutes.

3 Tip the dough into a mixer bowl and paddle on medium speed for 3–4 minutes until cooled slightly. With the mixer on medium, add the beaten eggs, in small amounts until you have a smooth, thick, shiny paste; you may only need 2½ eggs. It is the right consistency when a dollop holds a hooked peak. Spoon the choux pastry into a plastic bag, seal and snip off one corner to make a 2cm diameter hole for piping.

4 Pipe a choux ring just outside the outline on the paper, then pipe another concentric ring outside it, closely so they are touching. Pipe 2 rings on top and another on top of the join. Smooth the joins with damp fingertips.

5 For the glaze, beat the egg with the salt, then gently brush over the top and sides of the choux. Bake for 15 minutes, then reduce the setting to 180°C/Gas 4. Bake for a further 20–25 minutes or until the choux ring is golden brown, puffed and cooked through. Switch off the oven and leave the choux inside with the oven door slightly ajar to dry out for another 30 minutes. Transfer to a wire rack to cool.

6 For the filling, whip the cream in a large bowl until soft peaks form, then fold in the chocolate hazelnut spread. Spoon into a plastic bag, seal and snip off one corner.

7 Just before serving, halve the choux ring horizontally with a serrated knife and remove any wet dough from inside. Pipe most of the filling into the shell and sandwich together.

THE CREAMY CHOCOLATE AND HAZELNUT FILLING FOR THIS FRENCH
CHOUX DESSERT IS TOTALLY ADDICTIVE. KENTISH COBNUTS ONLY HAVE
A SHORT SEASON BUT YOU CAN, OF COURSE, SUBSTITUTE HAZELNUTS.

TO PLATE

Pipe the remaining chocolate cream into the centre of the Paris Brest. Top with cobnuts and dust with icing sugar. Drizzle a little vanilla syrup around the plate, if you like.

TO PLATE

Using a paintbrush, smear a stroke of chocolate
on one side of each plate. Dust the brownies
with icing sugar and place one on each plate.
Scoop the sorbet into small pots, sprinkle with
vanilla salt and serve on the side.

Chocolate brownie with vanilla salt and chocolate sorbet

SERVES **4**

CHOCOLATE BROWNIE:
210g butter, plus extra to grease the tin
320g good-quality dark chocolate
100g plain flour
80g cocoa powder
4 large eggs
260g caster sugar

VANILLA SALT:
2 tbsp sea salt
1 vanilla pod, split lengthways

TO SERVE:
20g chocolate, melted, to paint the plates
icing sugar, to dust
Chocolate sorbet (see page 182)

1 Preheat the oven to 180°C/Gas 4. Grease a 20cm square baking tin and line with baking parchment, leaving a slight overhang on each side to act as handles. Grease the parchment with butter.

2 Melt the chocolate and butter together in a heatproof bowl set over a pan of simmering water. Sift the flour and cocoa powder together into a small bowl.

3 Using an electric mixer, whisk the eggs and sugar together until the mixture is pale and thick enough to form a ribbon trail when the beaters are lifted, about 7–10 minutes. Carefully fold in the flour and cocoa mixture, using a rubber spatula.

4 Pour in a quarter of the melted chocolate mixture and fold together. Repeat until all of the chocolate is fully incorporated.

5 Pour the mixture into the prepared tin. Bake for 15–20 minutes until the top is firm to the touch. Leave to cool in the tin on a wire rack.

6 For the vanilla salt, put the salt into a small bowl. Scrape the sticky seeds from the vanilla pod and add them to the bowl. Mix with the salt, using your fingers.

7 When cool, lift the brownie out of the tin onto a board, using the paper handles. Now, using a serrated knife dipped in hot water, cut the brownie into slices.

THIS HAS THE PURE INTENSE CHOCOLATE HIT OF A CLASSIC BROWNIE, WITHOUT ANY NUTS OR DRIED FRUIT AS A DISTRACTION. THE VANILLA SALT ADDS A DELICATE TOUCH AND IS A GOOD FOIL FOR THE SWEET CHOCOLATE; IT'S A PAIRING I WAS INTRODUCED TO IN SPAIN.

Chocolate pots with star anise and biscotti

SERVES **4–6**

475ml double cream
70g caster sugar
pinch of salt
2 star anise pods
6 large egg yolks
225g good-quality dark chocolate

ALMOND BISCOTTI:
1 large egg
1 tsp vanilla extract
1 tsp almond extract
150g plain flour, plus extra to dust
½ tsp baking powder
pinch of salt
80g caster sugar
40g blanched whole almonds, coarsely chopped
1 egg white, lightly beaten
icing sugar, to dust

1 First, make the biscotti. Preheat the oven to 150°C/Gas 2 and line a baking sheet with greaseproof paper. In a small bowl, beat the egg with the vanilla and almond extracts. Sift the flour, baking powder and salt together into a larger bowl and stir in 70g of the sugar. Gradually incorporate the egg mix, mixing with your hands to a rough dough. Knead in the chopped almonds until evenly distributed.

2 Turn the dough onto a lightly floured surface and roll into a log, about 10cm in length. Brush the top with the egg white and sprinkle with the remaining sugar. Place on the prepared baking sheet and bake for 20–25 minutes until firm to the touch. Carefully lift onto a wire rack and leave to cool for about 5 minutes.

3 While the biscotti is still hot, transfer to a board and cut into 1cm thick slices. Place cut side up on a lined baking sheet and bake for 5–7 minutes. Turn the slices over and bake for another 5–7 minutes until firm to touch. Transfer to a wire rack and leave to cool. Store any extra biscotti in an airtight container.

4 To make the chocolate pots, pour the cream into a heavy-based saucepan and add the sugar, salt and star anise. Slowly bring to the boil and then remove from the heat. In a large bowl, whisk the egg yolks. Now gradually pour the hot cream mixture onto the yolks, whisking all the time.

5 Pour the mixture back into the pan and place over a low heat. Cook gently, stirring constantly with a wooden spoon until the custard is thick enough to coat the back of the spoon. Take off the heat and leave to infuse for 15 minutes.

6 Meanwhile, melt the chocolate in a heatproof bowl set over a pan of simmering water. Stir until smooth and set aside.

7 Remove the star anise from the custard and gradually stir in the melted chocolate. Pour into small serving bowls and chill until set, about 30 minutes.

IF YOU ARE LOOKING FOR A DESSERT THAT IS QUICK TO MAKE, THIS IS THE ONE FOR YOU. IT WILL CERTAINLY SATISFY ANY CHOCOLATE CRAVINGS.

Dust the biscotti lightly with icing sugar. Serve each chocolate pot with a little pile of biscotti.

Sprinkle the grated almonds on top of the raspberries and add a drizzle of vanilla syrup, if you like. Set the glasses on plates with some fresh raspberries to one side, scattered with mint leaves.

White chocolate custard with raspberries

SERVES **4**

140ml double cream
50ml milk
175g good-quality white chocolate, chopped
2 large egg yolks, beaten
100g raspberries
4 tbsp thick natural yoghurt

TO FINISH:
4 blanched almonds, grated (ideally on a microplane)
Vanilla syrup (see page 180), to drizzle (optional)
100g raspberries
mint leaves

1 Put the cream and milk into a small heavy-based saucepan over a medium-low heat until simmering. Place the white chocolate in a heatproof bowl and slowly pour the hot cream mixture over it. Let stand for 2 minutes, then stir until completely melted and smooth.

2 Pour the mixture back into the pan and stir with a wooden spoon over a low heat until it thickens enough to lightly coat the back of the spoon. Strain the custard through a fine sieve into a jug. Pour into 4 stemmed glasses and chill until set.

3 Place the raspberries in a small bowl and lightly crush them with a fork.

4 When ready to serve, top each chocolate custard with a spoonful of raspberries and a dollop of yoghurt.

HERE THE SHARPNESS OF THE RASPBERRIES CUTS
THE RICHNESS OF THE WHITE CHOCOLATE PERFECTLY.
GRATED ALMONDS ADD A LOVELY FINISHING TOUCH.

Unmould each delice by gently warming the ring mould in your hands or very briefly with a cook's blowtorch and releasing onto a serving plate. Top each delice with a neat spoonful of pear purée and a rolled pear slice. Place a few spoonfuls of pear purée and rolled pear slices around the plate. Drizzle with the tea syrup and finish with the reserved vanilla pods.

Chocolate delice with pear purée and jasmine tea syrup

SERVES **4–6**

BASE:

15g good-quality white chocolate

20g chocolate hazelnut spread, such as Nutella

8g vegetable suet

25g cornflakes cereal

MOUSSE:

80g good-quality dark chocolate

1 large egg yolk

30g caster sugar

140ml double cream

20ml milk

4 tsp Chocolate sorbet (see page 182)

PEAR PURÉE AND PEAR SLICES:

2 firm, ripe pears

1 tsp lemon juice

½ vanilla pod, split lengthways and
   seeds scraped

1 tsp brown sugar

TEA SYRUP:

1 tsp jasmine tea

80g caster sugar

½ vanilla pod, split lengthways and
   seeds scraped

1 To make the base, melt the white chocolate, hazelnut spread and suet together in a heatproof bowl set over a pan of barely simmering water. Stir until smooth, take off the heat and mix in the cornflakes. Put the mixture into a strong plastic bag and seal, excluding as much air as possible. Roll out, crushing the cereal, to make a thin sheet. Place in the fridge to firm up, about 15 minutes. Unwrap and lay on a work surface. Using a 4–5cm pastry cutter, cut out rounds from the base. (Save the trimmings – to crush and use as a topping for ice creams.)

2 For the mousse, melt the chocolate in a heat-bowl set over a pan of simmering water; remove and keep warm. Whisk the egg yolk and sugar together in a large heatproof bowl over the simmering water until foamy and light (the mixture should reach 74°C). Let cool slightly.

3 Softly whip the cream with the milk, then gradually fold in the melted chocolate, then the whisked yolk mix. Put into a plastic bag, seal and snip off one corner to make a piping tip.

4 Set 4–6 ring moulds, 4–5cm in diameter, on a tray and place a base round in each. Pipe in enough mousse to half-fill, then using a melon baller, put a small scoop of sorbet in the middle, making sure it doesn't touch the sides. Fill with the rest of the mousse and level the tops. Place in the freezer for at least 1 hour to set.

5 For the pear purée and slices, halve the pears and finely slice one pear half, with a mandolin if possible. Place the slices in a bowl and gently toss with the lemon juice. Cover and chill.

6 Core the remaining pear halves, then purée in a blender. Tip into a saucepan and add the vanilla seeds (reserving the pod) and brown sugar. Cook, stirring, over a medium-low heat until slightly thickened, about 3–4 minutes. Pour into a bowl, cover and chill.

7 To make the tea syrup, put the tea, sugar, 80ml water and the vanilla seeds and pod into another pan. Bring to the boil, stirring to dissolve the sugar, then set aside to cool.

THIS TRENDY, CHEFFY DESSERT TAKES MORE TIME THAN MOST
OF MY DESSERTS BUT IT CERTAINLY HAS THAT WOW FACTOR.

Chocolate cheesecake

MAKES **8–10** SLICES

BASE:

35g butter, plus extra to grease the tin

130g digestive biscuits, crushed

15g caster sugar

FILLING:

180g good-quality dark chocolate

470g cream cheese

190g caster sugar

6 large egg yolks, beaten

2 tsp vanilla extract

3 pinches of salt

700g soured cream

CHOCOLATE CURLS:

50g good-quality dark chocolate

1 Preheat the oven to 180°C/Gas 4. Lightly butter a 20cm springform cake tin and line the bottom with buttered greaseproof paper. Scrunch a sheet of foil under the base and around the outside of the tin (to prevent any water seeping in during baking).

2 For the base, melt the butter in a small pan. Put the biscuits into a strong plastic bag and crush with a rolling pin, then tip into a bowl. Stir in the sugar, then the melted butter, until evenly combined. Scatter in the prepared tin and press firmly with the base of a flat-bottomed glass. Place in the freezer to firm up.

3 For the filling, melt the chocolate in a heatproof bowl set over a pan of simmering water. Stir until smooth and set aside.

4 In a large bowl, mix the cream cheese and sugar together with a spatula until smooth. Slowly mix in the beaten egg yolks, then the vanilla extract and salt. Finally stir in the soured cream.

5 Pour half of the cheesecake filling over the base, then spoon in half of the chocolate. Now pour in the rest of the cheese mixture and top with the remaining chocolate. Swirl the chocolate through the cheese mixture, by drawing figure-of-eight patterns using a knife.

6 Stand the cake tin in a large roasting tin and pour in enough hot water to come about two-thirds of the way up the side of the cake tin. Bake in the oven for 45 minutes until the filling is just set. Switch off the oven and leave the cake inside to cool slowly as the oven cools down. Once cooled, transfer to the fridge and chill overnight.

7 To make the chocolate curls, hold the chocolate in your hands to warm it slightly, then using a vegetable peeler, shave off curls.

8 Run a thin knife around the edge of the cheesecake. Release the side of the tin and place the cake on a serving plate.

WHEN SPENDING TIME IN NEW YORK, YOU HAVE TO TRY THE AMAZING CHEESECAKES ON OFFER; MOST CHEFS DO THEIR OWN VERSION. HERE'S MY HOMAGE TO THE NY CHEESECAKE.

Scatter the chocolate curls on top of
the cheesecake to finish.

Slice the cake with a hot knife. Sift icing sugar over each slice before plating. Spoon some macerated raspberries on and around the cake and drizzle with some of the juice.

Spiced chocolate cake with macerated raspberries

MAKES **8–10** SLICES

200g unsalted butter, cut into cubes,
  plus extra to grease the dish
2 tbsp plain flour, plus extra to dust
¼ tsp ground ginger
¼ tsp ground allspice
¼ tsp ground cinnamon
200g good-quality dark chocolate, chopped
150g caster sugar
5 large eggs, separated

MACERATED RASPBERRIES:

250g raspberries
3 tbsp icing sugar, plus extra to dust
3 lemon thyme sprigs, leaves picked

1 First, prepare the macerated raspberries. In a bowl, whisk the icing sugar with 3 tbsp warm water until dissolved, then add the raspberries and lemon thyme leaves and toss gently. Set aside to macerate for an hour or so.

2 Preheat the oven to 180°C/Gas 4. Grease the base and sides of a 23cm Pyrex flan dish, 4cm deep, with butter and dust with flour, tapping out the excess.

3 Sift the 2 tbsp flour with the spices and set aside. Melt the chocolate and butter together in a heatproof bowl set over a pan of gently simmering water. Remove from the heat and stir in the sugar and spiced flour. Let cool slightly for a minute or two, then beat in the egg yolks until well combined.

4 In a clean bowl, whisk the egg whites with an electric whisk until soft peaks form. Using a rubber spatula, carefully fold into the chocolate mixture, a third at a time.

5 Pour the mixture into the prepared dish and bake for about 30 minutes until a cocktail stick inserted into the centre comes out with some moist crumbs attached. Leave in the dish to firm up a little, then transfer to a wire rack to cool slightly. The cake will rise and the top is likely to crack in the oven, then it will collapse slightly on cooling.

IF, LIKE ME, YOU ARE INTO CHOCOLATE, YOU WILL LOVE THE RICHNESS OF THIS CAKE. GENTLY SPICED WITH CINNAMON, GINGER AND ALLSPICE, IT IS BEAUTIFULLY MOIST AND VERY EASY TO MAKE.

basics

Vanilla sugar syrup

MAKES ABOUT 250ML
100g caster sugar
1 vanilla pod

1 Put the sugar and 200ml water in a small saucepan over a low heat. When the sugar has dissolved, increase the heat and bring to the boil. Split the vanilla pod lengthways, scrape out the seeds and add them to the sugar syrup. (Save the pod to make vanilla sugar.)

2 Take off the heat and leave the syrup to cool. Store in a jar or bottle in the fridge and use as required. It will keep for a week or two.

Vanilla sugar: Immerse vanilla pods
in a jar of caster sugar and they will infuse the sugar with their fragrance. You can use empty pods that have been scraped of their seeds; rinse and dry well if the pods have been infused in a liquid, such as a custard.

Vanilla crème anglaise

MAKES ABOUT 300ML
125ml double cream
125ml whole milk
1 vanilla pod
35g caster sugar
3 large egg yolks

1 Put the cream and milk into a heavy-based saucepan. Split the vanilla pod lengthways and scrape out the seeds with the back of the knife. Add these to the pan along with the empty pod and heat slowly until it is almost starting to boil. Take off the heat and set aside to infuse for 10 minutes.

2 Beat the sugar and egg yolks together in a large bowl until smooth and creamy. Pour the warm vanilla cream onto the egg mix, whisking to combine, then pour this mixture through a fine sieve into the cleaned saucepan. Stir continuously over a low heat, using a wooden spoon, until thickened to a thin custard, which will lightly coat the back of the spoon; do not allow to boil. Immediately pour into a bowl.

3 If you're not using the custard straight away, cool it down quickly by setting the bowl in a larger bowl of iced water. Stir occasionally to prevent a skin from forming. Chill and use within a few days.

Vanilla ice cream

SERVES 6–8
250ml double cream
250ml whole milk
2 vanilla pods
100g caster sugar
6 large egg yolks

1 Pour the cream and milk into a heavy-based saucepan. Split the vanilla pods lengthways and scrape out the seeds with the back of a knife. Add both the seeds and pods to the pan and slowly bring to the boil.

2 Meanwhile, beat the sugar and egg yolks together in a bowl. As soon as the creamy milk bubbles up the side of the pan, remove from the heat and slowly trickle the liquid onto the sugary yolks, beating well. When fully incorporated, pour the mixture back into the cleaned pan and stir over a medium-low heat with a wooden spoon until the mixture thickens enough to thinly coat the back of the spoon; do not allow to boil.

3 Leave to cool completely, then pass through a sieve into an ice-cream maker and churn until smooth and thick. Transfer to a freezerproof container, seal and freeze until needed.

Coconut sorbet

SERVES 4–6
500ml coconut milk
75g liquid glucose
40g icing sugar
2 tbsp coconut flavoured rum (Malibu)

1 Warm the coconut milk and 75ml water in a saucepan over a low heat. Add the liquid glucose and icing sugar and whisk until fully dissolved. Remove from the heat and stir in the rum. Pour into a bowl, cover and allow to cool.

2 Once cooled, pour into an ice-cream maker and churn until almost firm. Transfer to a suitable container, seal and place in the freezer until ready to serve. Best eaten within a week of making.

Chocolate sorbet

SERVES 4–6
50ml milk
75g caster sugar
20g liquid glucose
15g unsweetened cocoa powder
25g milk chocolate, chopped
25g dark, bitter chocolate, chopped

1 Put the milk, 200ml water, the sugar, liquid glucose and cocoa powder into a saucepan. Bring to the boil over a medium-high heat, stirring continuously with a whisk. Lower the heat and simmer gently for 2 minutes.

2 Take off the heat, add all the chopped chocolate and whisk for about 2 minutes until fully melted and smooth. Allow to cool.

3 Once cooled, pour the mixture into an ice-cream maker and churn until almost firm. Transfer to a suitable container, seal and place in the freezer until ready to serve. Best eaten within a week of making.

Strawberry sorbet

SERVES 4–6
750g strawberries, hulled
100g liquid glucose
50g icing sugar (approximately)
1 tbsp lemon juice (approximately)

1 Purée the strawberries in a blender, then pass through a fine sieve (preferably lined with muslin), pressing the pulp with the back of a ladle to extract as much juice as possible.

2 Pour the strawberry juice into a saucepan and warm over a low heat, then add the liquid glucose and icing sugar and whisk until completely dissolved. Remove from the heat and add the lemon juice. Taste for sweetness; you may need a little more icing sugar or lemon juice, depending on how sweet the strawberries are. Pour into a bowl, cover and allow to cool.

3 Once cooled, pour the mixture into an ice-cream maker and churn until almost firm. Transfer to a suitable container, seal and place in the freezer until ready to serve. Best eaten within a week of making.

Candied lime and lemon zest

MAKES ABOUT 50G
zest of 2 limes (in long strips)
zest of 2 lemons (in long strips)
100g caster sugar
30g granulated sugar

1 Bring a saucepan of water to the boil. Add the citrus zests and blanch for 1 minute, then drain. Repeat this process twice, changing the water each time.

2 Put the caster sugar and 100ml water into a saucepan over a low heat and stir to dissolve the sugar. Increase the heat, bring to the boil and let bubble for a minute or two. Add the citrus zests and simmer for about 3–5 minutes until softened.

3 Remove the citrus zest with a slotted spoon, discarding the syrup. Toss the zest strips in a small bowl with the granulated sugar to coat evenly, then place on a tray lined with baking parchment and let stand until dry, about 15 minutes.

Candied orange zest: Use the pared zest of 2 large oranges, in long strips, in place of the lime and lemon zest.

Apple purée

SERVES 4–6
4 Granny Smith apples
2 tsp lemon juice, or to taste
25g butter
caster sugar, to taste (optional)

1 Peel, halve and core the apples, then cut into dice and toss in 1 tsp lemon juice to prevent browning. Heat the butter in a frying pan over a low heat and sauté the apples until just starting to soften. Add the rest of the lemon juice and cook until the apples are completely soft; do not allow them to brown.

2 Tip the apples into a blender and purée until smooth. If the purée seems a little too thin, tip it back into the frying pan and stir over a medium-low heat to reduce and thicken slightly, about 5 minutes. Add a little caster sugar to taste, if you like. Transfer to a bowl or jar, cover and refrigerate. Use within 3 days.

Mayonnaise

MAKES ABOUT 300ML
2 large egg yolks
1 tsp Dijon mustard
sea salt and black pepper
275ml light olive oil
2 tsp white wine vinegar

1 Put the egg yolks, mustard and a little seasoning into a small food processor and whiz until thick and smooth. With the motor running, very slowly trickle in the olive oil. The mixture should be thick and creamy.

2 Add the wine vinegar, then adjust the seasoning. For a lighter consistency, thin the mayonnaise down with 1–2 tbsp warm water.

note: If the mixture curdles as you are adding the oil, transfer it to a jug and put another egg yolk into the food processor bowl. Start again, slowly blending the curdled mixture into the egg yolk, and the mayonnaise should re-emulsify.

Aïoli

MAKES ABOUT 200ML
pinch of saffron strands
4 garlic cloves, peeled and finely crushed
2 medium egg yolks
80g thick creamy mashed potato (optional)
150ml olive oil
sea salt and black pepper

1 Put the saffron, garlic, egg yolks and potato, if using, into a blender or food processor. Blend until the mixture is thick and smooth. With the motor running, slowly trickle in the olive oil until fully incorporated. Season well with salt and pepper.

2 Transfer the aïoli to a bowl or jar, cover and refrigerate. Use within 3 days.

Vinaigrette

MAKES 350ML
50ml white wine vinegar
300ml extra-virgin olive oil
sea salt and black pepper

1 Put all the ingredients into a jug and blitz, using a hand-held stick blender, to emulsify. Alternatively, shake in a screw-topped jar.

2 Store in the fridge for up to a week and shake well before each use.

Spicy ketchup

MAKES ABOUT 100G
90g tomato ketchup
15ml red wine vinegar
1 tsp Worcestershire sauce
7 drops of Tabasco sauce

1 In a small bowl, whisk together all of the ingredients.

2 Cover and refrigerate until ready to serve. Use within 3 days.

Chicken stock

MAKES ABOUT 1.5–2 LITRES
1.5kg chicken bones
1½ celery sticks, trimmed and roughly chopped
1 leek, white part only, trimmed and roughly
   chopped
2 onions, peeled and roughly chopped
¼ garlic bulb, unpeeled
1 thyme sprig

1 Put the chicken bones into a large stockpot and pour in just enough cold water to cover (about 3 litres). Bring to the boil and skim off the scum that rises to the surface, then turn the heat down as low as possible.

2 Add all the remaining ingredients, making sure they are all fully submerged in the water. Let the stock simmer for 3–4 hours, then pass it through a muslin-lined sieve into a bowl. Allow to cool.

3 If not using the stock immediately, cover, refrigerate and use within 5 days, or divide into convenient quantities and freeze in suitable containers.

Veal stock

MAKES ABOUT 1.5–2 LITRES
1.5kg veal or beef bones
75ml olive oil
1 large onion, peeled and roughly chopped
2 large carrots, peeled and roughly chopped
2 celery sticks, peeled and roughly chopped
¼ garlic bulb, unpeeled
1½ tbsp tomato purée
1 thyme sprig
1 bay leaf

1 Preheat the oven to 220°C/Gas 7. Put the veal bones in a roasting tin, drizzle with half the olive oil and roast in the oven for about 1 hour until golden brown.

2 Heat the remaining oil in a large stockpot and add the chopped vegetables and garlic. Stir frequently over a medium heat until the vegetables are lightly golden. Add the tomato purée and stir for another 2–3 minutes.

3 Add the browned veal bones to the stockpot, leaving behind the excess fat. Pour over enough cold water to cover, about 5 litres, and bring to a gentle simmer. Skim off any scum that rises to the surface. Add the thyme and bay leaf and let simmer for 5–6 hours.

4 Strain the stock through a muslin-lined sieve into a clean pan. Return to the heat and boil until reduced by half.

5 If not using immediately, allow to cool and freeze in batches, or refrigerate and use within 5 days.

Fish stock

MAKES ABOUT 1.5 LITRES

1.5kg white fish bones (such as plaice, sea
  bream or haddock), washed
2 tbsp olive oil
1 onion, peeled and roughly chopped
1 leek, white part only, trimmed and roughly
  chopped
1 celery stick, trimmed and roughly chopped
1 small fennel bulb, roughly chopped
3 garlic cloves, peeled
300ml white wine
1 bay leaf
1 thyme sprig
few parsley stalks
10 white peppercorns
1 lemon, sliced

1 Chop the fish bones into smaller pieces and
set aside. Heat the olive oil in a large stockpot
and sweat the onion, leek, celery, fennel and
garlic for 4–5 minutes. Pour in the white wine
and let bubble until reduced to a syrupy glaze.
Add the herbs, peppercorns, lemon slices and
fish bones to the pot.

2 Cover with 2 litres cold water and bring to a
simmer, skimming off the scum that rises to
the surface. Gently simmer for 20 minutes.

3 Allow the stock to cool and settle, then
strain it through a muslin-lined sieve. Freeze
in smaller quantities if not using at once, or
refrigerate and use within 2 or 3 days.

Vegetable stock

MAKES ABOUT 1.5 LITRES

5 carrots, trimmed and roughly chopped
2 onions, trimmed and roughly chopped
2 celery sticks, trimmed and roughly chopped
1 leek, white part only, trimmed and roughly
  chopped
few basil sprigs
few chervil sprigs
few chives
½ garlic bulb
2 star anise
6 coriander seeds
6 white peppercorns
6 pink peppercorns
200ml dry white wine
1 lemon, cut into wedges

1 Put the vegetables into a stockpot, cover
with 1.5–2 litres cold water and bring to the
boil. Lower the heat and simmer for about
10 minutes. Add the herbs, garlic and spices.
Simmer for a further 2 minutes, then add the
white wine and lemon wedges. Remove from
the heat and leave to cool completely.

2 Chill for 24 hours, dividing the stock into
smaller batches if the stockpot does not fit into
your fridge.

3 The following day, pass the stock through a
muslin-lined sieve. Freeze in smaller portions
if not using straightaway, or refrigerate and
use within 5 days.

Index

Acknowledgements

I am grateful to so many people who have worked tirelessly alongside me on this book – no one more so than Judy Joo, who had to put up with my ambitious recipes and make them work to a budget – no easy feat believe me. I genuinely appreciate the time and effort she has put into researching and testing these recipes.

A special thank you to Yuki Sugiura for the amazing photographs. Yuki has really captured the beauty of the food and has been terrific to work with. Thanks also to her assistant Linda Romppala, print processor Richard Chan, and stylist Cynthia Inions, who brought such perfect props to the shoots.

I would like to thank Janet Illsley for editing the book so carefully and putting in her much needed personal touches; Helen Lewis for designing and art directing the book in such a beautiful manner; and her assistant Nicola Davidson for all her hard work. Thanks also to Anne Furniss, for believing in this crazy project and her continuing support.

I am hugely grateful to my whole team of chefs who constantly inspire me with their dedication and hard work. We live in a crazy chef's world and I only add to the pressure when I ask them to help me on a project like this, yet they graciously take it in their stride. A big thank you to James Durrant, Paul Hood, Matt Bishop, Matt Laville, Angie Steele and Bashir Lintzmeyer.

Project director Anne Furniss
Creative director Helen Lewis
Project editor Janet Illsley
Photographer Yuki Sugiura
Recipe testing Judy Joo
Props stylist Cynthia Inions
Designer Nicola Davidson
Production Vincent Smith, Aysun Hughes

First published in 2010 by
Quadrille Publishing Limited
Alhambra House, 27–31 Charing Cross
Road, London WC2H 0LS
www.quadrille.co.uk

Reprinted in 2010
10 9 8 7 6 5 4 3 2

Text © 2010 Jason Atherton
Photography © 2010 Yuki Sugiura
Design and layout © 2010 Quadrille
Publishing Limited

The rights of the author have been asserted.

Cataloguing in Publication Data: a catalogue record for this book is available from the British Library.

ISBN 978 184400 816 2

Printed in China